The Economic Consequences of the Gulf War

The Gulf War ranks in terms of scale of destruction and its consequent economic impact as one of the most devestating conflicts of modern times. Both Iran and Iraq are now confronted with the need to reconstruct shattered economies. What is clear, however, is that a return to the pre-war economic situation is not a realistic option. The cost of the conflict to Iraq means that it can never regain the lead it formerly held in economic performance and development levels. Similarly, the Islamic Republic cannot return to economic principles of the Shah's regime. What, then, does reconstruction mean?

In *The Economic Consequences of the Gulf War*, Kamran Mofid details the formerly neglected costs of the conflict to both Iraq and Iran and to the region as a whole. The catastrophic effect of the conflict on the economies of Iran and Iraq is examined, looking in particular at its impact on oil production and exports, foreign exchange earnings and foreign trade, and agricultural performance. Case studies of the militarization of each country are provided, with pre-war data included for comparative purposes.

In exposing the pyrrhic nature of the Gulf War the author raises some crucial issues. Although the terminology of ceasefire has centred on the idea of reconstruction he questions the immediate future of the region, pointing out that regional stability is an essential pre-condition to the process of rebuilding.

The Author
Kamran Mofid is Senior Lecturer in Economics at Coventry Polytechnic, and is the author of *Development Planning in Iran: From Monarchy to Islamic Republic*.

The Economic Consequences of the Gulf War

Kamran Mofid

London and New York

First published 1990 by Routledge
11 New Fetter Lane, London EC4P 4EE

Simultaneously published in the USA and Canada
by Routledge
a division of Routledge, Chapman and Hall, Inc.
29 West 35th Street, New York, NY 10001

© 1990 K. Mofid

Typeset by J&L Composition Ltd, Filey, North Yorkshire

Printed and bound in Great Britain by
Mackays of Chatham PLC, Chatham, Kent

British Library Cataloguing in Publication Data
Mofid, Kamran
 The Economic Consequences of the Gulf War.
 1. Iran. Economic Conditions   2. Iraq. Economic conditions
 I. Title
 330.955054

 ISBN 0–415–05295–5

Library of Congress Cataloging in Publication Data
Mofid, Kamran.
 The Economic Consequences of the Gulf War. / Kamran Mofid.
  p.   cm.
 Includes bibliographical references.
 ISBN 0–415–05295–5
 1. Iran–Defenses–Economic aspects.   2. Iraq–defenses–Economic
 aspects.   3. Iran–Iraq War, 1980–1988–Economic aspects.   I. Title.
 HC480.D4M64   1990
 955.05′4–dc20   90–31657
                                                                CIP

For my Father and Mother

Contents

Contents

Figures

ix

Tables

Tables

Tables

Foreword

The Iran–Iraq war may indeed be reaching the end of its turbulent and destructive road. The blood may have stopped flowing – for the moment – but the long march towards recovery – at a high price for the civilian population of both countries – has hardly begun. It is indicative of the extent and level of destruction, and the intensity of an 'old' conflict fought with the most up-to-date weapons that our 'modern' (competing) civilizations of East and West have manufactured, that the terminology of the ceasefire period has centred around such ill-defined (but thankfully un-ideological) vagaries as reconstruction, rejuvenation, rebuilding, etc. The concept 'development', defined by the orthodox political economists as the process of modernizing economic structures and processes and catching-up with the advanced capitalist countries, has been shelved in this northern Gulf region, perhaps in response to the makeshift and unplanned strategies favoured by the belligerents themselves for two broad reasons. First, as Dr Mofid illustrates in this book, because, while these protagonists have been busy destroying each other's economies and the very fabric of their national infrastructures, the rest of the developing world has been preoccupied with the simultaneous struggle to weather and capitalize on the tantrums of the world economy and to get on with the difficult task of creating and consolidating modern industries and economies. Second, and more to the point, it appears that the direct and indirect destruction inflicted upon the two economies is such that it may actually be cognitively misleading to refer to the post-ceasefire economic processes in Iran and Iraq as anything but 'reconstruction'. Technically, 'development', the cumulative process of industrialization and modernization, may as yet not be occurring.

But what does reconstruction mean? 'Going back' (i.e. rebuilding) to the 1980 economic situation in the two countries? Surely not! Observers of the Persian Gulf region will be aware that, at that time, Iran's socio-economic system had reached near-collapse, and that (as all the major economic indices show) her economy was functioning at under 40 per cent of capacity. Moreover, it can hardly be the case that the rulers of the Islamic Republic of Iran, having presided over the nearly complete annihilation of what was Pahlavi Iran, would now be willing to recreate the same (i.e. not even similar) structures once again. Although it can be argued that closer examination does show that the ruling mullahs and their technocratic servants have not really even attempted to change the fundamentals of the Pahlavi economic system, it is clear that they, and the country as a whole, will be unable to flourish if the return to the Pahlavi system is the agenda.

In Iraq's case also the 'going back' is an unrealizable ideal, for three main reasons:

(i) the country owes too prohibitive an amount of money to other countries today for her to have the complete independence of action essential for recapturing the lead she has lost in Arab economic performance and development levels,

(ii) the level of military expenditures and the political instabilities associated with them currently inhibit national expenditure levels achieved in the 'golden decade' of the 1970s,

(iii) almost complete dependence on the international price of oil and petroleum exports makes nonsense of any careful planning and target assignments in the current situation, unlike that which was set and achieved in the last decade.

It is pertinent to ask therefore that, if reconstruction does not denote a return to the prewar era, then what does it amount to? I believe that, as this war has produced neither a victor nor vanquished, and consequently, as both regimes have remained intact, reconstruction must, in the last analysis, only mean restrengthening. More precisely, it is feasible and probable that a long period of competitive restrengthening, stemming from mutual distrust, fear and regional ambitions, may have already been institutionalized. But, to grasp fully the basis of competitive restrengthening, we must systematically evaluate the lessons and legacies of this war in its domestic context, regional consequences, international perceptions and historical precedences.

Domestic context

Domestically, the pressures to militarize, which were in evidence in the 1970s, have increased, expanding both the role of the military in national political life, and their consumption ration in the national budget. Furthermore, the fact that the two regimes have remained in power without gaining any tangible results from the war merely enhances their domestic positions *vis-à-vis* the disgruntled civilian populations and their respective national and ethnic adversaries. Without checks and balances within the political system, and in the absence of constructive debate on issues of national importance in both countries, the regimes in power are able not only to define the threats, but also to mobilize their populations in the required direction and continue to bypass the legitimate demands of the masses for a better quality of life. Under these conditions, war will give the protagonists a chance to test their strengths and weaknesses, and peace an opportunity to re-arm, consolidate and prepare for further clashes: in other words, the institutionalization of functional instability *par excellence*.

Regional consequences

Regionally, the Iran–Iraq war has produced very interesting by-products; its commencement led to the creation of the Gulf Co-operation Council in 1981, and its (imminent?) termination has given birth to the Arab Co-operation Council (ACC) in 1989. The former was the reaction of the Southern Gulf states to the war, and the latter the result of the Iraqi war effort and the military support it received from within the region. Iraq's ACC partners, Jordan, Egypt and North Yemen, are the same countries which consistently supported the Iraqi war effort; Jordan and Egypt offered military manpower, Jordan provided a safer land route for the beleaguered Iraqis, and all three supplied arms, ammunition and support systems.

On another scene, the Iran–Iraq war forced the regional hands of the important Arab and non-Arab states in the complex game of power politics in this sub-system's microcosms. Syria, Libya and South Yemen abandoned their erstwhile radical ally – Iraq – in favour of the Islamic Iran. Israel, Syria's most immediate regional enemy, also supported the Iranian war effort against Iraq, which, as already mentioned, received uncritical support from a number of key moderate Arab countries including Egypt – the only Arab state with diplomatic ties to Israel. So, in this circus of short-term alliances, undercover partnerships and bizarre contractual agreements, enemies from one regional theatre became objective bedfellows in the Persian Gulf politico-military crisis, and politico-ideological allies on key regional issues (on the Arab–Israeli conflict, Palestinian statehood and the Camp David Accords, for instance) ended up objective enemies in the respective Iraq–Iran war 'supporters clubs'. More disturbing, within the regional context, is the perseverance of these opportunistic musical-chairs tendencies since the ceasefire in the Iran–Iraq war. Syrian, Israeli, Iranian and now Iraqi involvement in Lebanese politics and factional fightings illustrates well the dangers associated with such loose loyalties. The living tragedies of the Lebanese situation help to explain its consequences.

International perceptions

In its international dimension the Iran–Iraq war has been declared one of the longest uninterrupted wars between modern nation-states since 1945. Dr Mofid's efforts incidentally help to explain why it may also prove to have been one of the costliest since records began.

The increased dependence of the belligerents on outside material and moral support provided unforeseen opportunities (and as it turned out pitfalls as well) for extra-regional countries and forces to expand their influence in this oil- and natural-gas-rich part of the world. In many ways the decline in the influence of the American and Soviet superpowers in Iran and Iraq respectively, particularly after 1980, was a function of the expansion of other countries' involvement in Persian Gulf affairs. But the protagonists had set different criteria for the demonstration of their commitment to the party of their choice. Iraq expected diplomatic and economic support and isolation of Iran in exchange for 'favours'. Iran, on the other hand, insisted on barter deals and badly needed arms, ammunition and communication equipment. Many countries chose to satisfy both parties' demands by openly objecting to the war, on the one hand, and secretly supplying Iran with the range of American- and Western-European-made arms deployed by her regular and revolutionary armed forces on the other. Some others preferred to push for a significant market share in either one country. Vietnam, Sweden, South Africa and the two Koreas fall into this category, as far as the Iranian market is concerned. France and the Soviet Union, of course, had major military interests to protect in Iraq. But the most startling aspect of this war's 'international connection' is the fact that at one time or another nearly one-third of the United Nations membership was involved in providing either weapons, ammunition or support systems to both belligerents simultaneously, undermining totally the integrity of the United Nations (UN) system as an independent arbiter and the collective conscience of the community of nations.

It is ironic that the prime movers behind the UN Security Council Resolution 598 – the permanent members of the council – which led to the Gulf War ceasefire in July 1988 are all also on that list of countries which have supplied weapons and support systems to both parties to the conflict!

The political and ideological mix of the countries that have been capitalizing on the misfortunes of Iran and Iraq supports the theory of global power-bloc decomposition as alluded to in the previous paragraph. The close – and at times intimate – military support and assistance obtained by the belligerents from the bewildering range of political 'authorities and systems' shows that the military collaborations were not based on ideological position and the pursuit of power-bloc politics. Indeed, if anything, the pattern of arms suppliers to the two warring countries indicates that either the superpowers were using their proxies to supply the belligerents; or the superpowers had lost control of their allies and proxies in this case; and/or the East–West global divide had actually been breaking down at the seams, thus enabling the two blocs' 'part-time' proxies to pursue an independent line based purely on their national interests and motives. If the latter is the case, then international support for the various parties to other regional wars may follow a similar pattern of dangerous 'pragmatic' international relations which at the very least help to prolong war and increase the sufferings of the societies concerned and, at worst, encourage internationalization of a local conflict in the absence of power-bloc pressures and policy directives. The fact that Marxist Vietnam and Marxist China, ɛnemies in the Far East, both supported the anti-Marxist and overtly religious Iranian regime in its 'reactionary war' against Soviet-supported Ba'ath Socialist Iraq provides little comfort for those seeking political solutions and unideological approaches to international relations.

The international lessons of the Iran–Iraq war point also to another field of investigation, namely that, while the international system has been looking for ways of unlocking the East–West ideological door to regional conflict resolution, it has managed to overlook the difficulties and instabilities arising from differences from within each ideological divide and global heterogeneity. The Iranian revolution was the first in the contemporary world to break out of the socialist versus capitalist global mould and her war with Iraq provided further evidence of this trend and its other facets. A short reference to the attitudes of the self-declared Marxist-Leninist states towards the war shows that the three 'poles' of the International Communist Movement, the Soviet Union, China and Albania, adopted positions not only contrary to their own doctrines but squarely in opposition to their ideological competitors' interests, regardless of the international repercussions of their positions and actions. Albania concluded that Iran's position amounted to 'anti-imperialism' and she should therefore be supported in the war. China was seeking badly needed foreign exchange, profitable economic relations and ways of limiting Soviet influence – and indeed (if feasible) of hurting the Soviet position – and so ended up strongly supporting Iran. And the Soviet Union vacillated between countering the latent threat from an unstable and hostile Iran to her southern border and Muslim republics, and the need to support and protect her only long-standing Persian Gulf ally, Iraq, regardless of the maxims of the state's official ideology.

The divisions within the Western camp are more readily classifiable; all the parties, with the exception of the United States, France and the United Kingdom were interested solely in expanding their commercial and trade ties with the belligerents, their aim: sell everything that the protagonists needed, including the means of obtaining an unconventional weapons capability. The three named countries, however, were playing a more complex game of foreign policy, combining politics, commercial and security interests and strategic concerns within the same formula.

Historical precedences

Beyond these observations what historical precedences has this war set? First, it was allowed to continue at a fairly intensive level by the belligerents themselves in the first instance, and outside forces in the second. For years everyone found a reward in this war and, so long as this perception persisted, concerted efforts to end the conflict were diluted by either impossible demands, unacceptable propositions or outdated proposals. Second, weaponry of the highest order were used by both protagonists. Although deployed inefficiently at times, the weapons utilized were amongst the most sophisticated available, routinely deployed by the world's great and major powers alike. The ease with which both sides obtained and deployed complex and sophisticated weapons systems indicates that other Third World armies stockpiling similar weapons can easily annihilate those parties without them, thus encouraging regional arms races by the main actors involved 'to catch up and keep up'. Or else, if all parties deploy such complex and advanced weapons systems, then any ensuing war will be highly destructive and, if the supply routes are maintained and technical assistance channels present, long in duration as well. Third, the calculated deployment of chemical weapons and the indiscriminate firing of surface-to-surface missiles on civilian targets have qualitatively raised the mode and accepted levels of warfare in regional theatres, thus increasing the dangers of escalation and the problems associated with conflict management. And finally, on a more positive note, this war has shown that, when the constructive will of the international community, as embodied in the increased efforts of the UN, coincides with the exhaustion of one or more of the parties to a conflict, then formulating peace can become a remarkably straightforward affair. The ending of the war though and the conditions that have emerged in the region since July/ August 1988 point towards an unsettled future and one that leans more towards confrontation in the long term than compromise. The Iran–Iraq war, it seems, is only the beginning of the long road towards long-term peace, a peace that will be based on mutual respect, extensive interdependence and substantial co-operation. If we judge by the history of Europe, there will be many many other wars and antagonisms in the Persian Gulf before any real peace between all the parties can emerge. Moreover, it took Europe two world wars in the twentieth century and the dismembering of a powerful continental power (Germany), and many other continental wars besides, as well as the spectre of an invasion by a powerful and *common* enemy, before state violence was eventually erased from the agenda of inter-state relations of the Western European countries. The Western Europeans have paid a very high price for their current state of stable peace and co-ordinated and co-operative relations, as exemplified in the European Community and European Free Trade Association. It is tempting to prescribe similar solutions for eradicating the current structural problems that led to hostilities in the Persian Gulf region without taking account of the tortuous road towards the current European environment. But the geostrategic values of the Gulf to the superpowers and the dependence of developed and developing countries on its natural resources may cause such a massive regional and international competition for the full control of this region that the question of locally based co-operation agreements and the eventual unity of purpose may never even see the light of day – that is, if the nuclear winter sets in.

Anoushiravan Ehteshami
September 1989

Acknowledgements

I should like to express my sincere thanks for the help I received while writing this book. My wife, Annie, and my sons, Kevin and Paul, are at the top of the list. This is simply to express my deep gratitude for their immeasurable support and love over the years. They so kindly tolerated my withdrawal from family life from time to time and put up with my travels to close and faraway places so many times. Their overall love and care for me provided the environment in which to write and still remain myself.

I would also like to thank my father and mother – to whom I am dedicating this book – for their constant love and prayers. They encouraged me to continue my education and for that I am grateful.

I presented earlier drafts of some of the chapters of this book at different conferences and seminars. I am most grateful to those academic colleagues who commented on my work. As ever, they are absolved from all blame for the final outcome of my work, but they can be assured that this study is certainly better than it would have been without their contributions. In particular, I would like to thank Mr T. Hamauzu, Senior Research Officer, International Exchange Department, Institute of Developing Economies, Tokyo, for inviting me to Japan to present papers on the political economy of the Gulf War at the Institute in Tokyo and other establishments in Japan. I found my experience in, and of, Japan most rewarding. I would also like to thank Dr Gari Donn, the organizer, US–European Summer School on Global Security and Arms Control, University of Sussex, for inviting me to the School for the 1987 and 1988 sessions, and enabling me to share my research interests of the political economy of the Gulf with the other participants.

I should like to thank my academic colleagues at the British Society for Middle Eastern Studies and the Development Studies Association, for their comments on, and criticism of the topics relating to this study which I presented at the annual conferences.

I would also like to thank Messrs B. Moain, S. Radpour and B. Afagh of the BBC World Service, for inviting me on several occasions to speak on the Persian Service and share my findings with the people of Iran.

I should like to thank my colleagues at the Polytechnic for their support and encouragement; in particular Keith Redhead who so kindly and enthusiastically proof-read the entire manuscript and Dr D. Morris, Dean, Faculty of Business, and Clive Collis, Head, Department of Economics, for making it possible for me to have an extended leave so that I could travel to Japan. I would also like to thank Sue Joshua, Caroline Wintersgill and Rob Tarling of Routledge for their assistance in the final preparation of the book.

Finally, I must record my debt to the typists in the Typing Bureau at the Polytechnic, especially to Valerie Tyman and Betty Fox; without their help in converting my scrawl into a readable form, it would have taken me much much longer to finish this book.

Chapter one

Introduction

In September 1980 the Iraqi army invaded Iran. From that moment onwards the war and its consequences have intermittently been a focal point of world attention. Many articles and books have been written analysing mainly the historical, socio-political, military and religious/cultural aspects of the conflict, with its national, regional and international implications.[1]

Yet it is striking that the war, which in terms of scale of destruction and its consequent economic impact ranks as one of the most devastating conflicts since World War II, has not sufficiently caught the eyes and the imaginations of economists.[2] The analysis of the economic consequences of the Gulf War has received very scant coverage.

Furthermore it should be emphasized that it is the economic factors that have given rise to the paramount significance and importance of the war in general, and the Persian Gulf in particular.

Among the most important economic factors to be noted is that the combined proven oil reserves of the Gulf countries are the highest in the world. Iran, Iraq, Kuwait, Saudi Arabia, the United Arab Emirates (UAE) and Qatar together account for 56.9 per cent of the world's proven oil reserves. They also account for 25 per cent of the world's proven natural gas reserves, the highest in the non-communist world (see further tables 1.1 and 1.2).

Moreover, since the discovery of oil, the dependency of the outside world on imported oil from the Gulf has been increasing at a rapid rate. For example, North America's oil-import dependency has increased from 6.4 per cent in 1950 to 36.7 per cent in 1986, with most of the imports originating from the Gulf countries (see further tables 1.3 and 1.4).

It should further be noted that, the ratio of oil reserves to production (R/P) in most of the non-Gulf oil producers has fallen rapidly. For example, the R/P ratio in the United States of

1

Table 1.1   Proven oil reserves, 1 January 1987: the world and selected major areas (million tonnes)

		Share of the world total (%)*
World total	96,076	100.0
USA	3,351	3.5
Soviet Union	8,049	8.4
UK	1,330	1.4
Norway	1,432	1.5
Iran	6,658	6.9
Iraq	6,426	6.7
Kuwait	12,895	13.4
Saudi Arabia	23,396	24.4
UAE	4,508	5.0
Qatar	430	0.5

Note: * Author's calculation.
Source: *Statistiques* 1986

Table 1.2   Proven natural-gas reserves, 1 January 1987: the world and selected major areas (trillion cubic metres)

		Share of the world total (%)*
World total	102,739	100.0
USA	5,250	5.1
Canada	2,820	2.7
Norway	2,922	2.8
Netherlands	1,993	1.9
UK	946	0.9
Soviet Union	43,900	42.7
Iran	12,743	12.4
Iraq	793	0.8
Kuwait	1,166	1.1
Saudi Arabia	3,686	3.6
UAE	2,963	2.9
Qatar	4,304	4.2

Note: * Author's calculation.
Source: *Statistiques* 1986

America (USA) has fallen significantly from 11.1 years in 1970 to 9.5 years in 1980, 8.7 years in 1985 and 7.6 years in 1986,[3] which undoubtedly will affect the USA crude-oil dependency in the not too distant future.

Indeed, in a report concerning oil security in the US prepared in 1986 by the US Energy Department for President Reagan, it is projected that by 1995 the USA will be importing more than 60 per cent of its oil needs. The report also notes that at least half the non-Communist world's oil imports will originate from the Persian Gulf. (*MEED*, 31 October 1987:5).

Table 1.3 World oil production and consumption by major areas: 1950–86 (selected years) (million barrels per day)

	Production					Consumption				
	1950	1973	1978	1983	1986	1950	1973	1978	1983	1986
North America	6.2	13.6	13.3	11.7	12.0	6.6 (6.4)	19.6	21.4	15.6	16.4 (36.7)
Western Europe	0.1	0.5	1.8	3.4	4.0	1.3	15.2	14.3	11.5	11.7
Japan	–	–	–	–	–	0.1	5.5	5.4	4.2	4.1
Middle East	1.8	21.0	21.3	12.1	13.0	0.2	1.3	1.9	2.3	2.2

Sources: BP Statistical Review of World Energy 1987 and Shell Briefing Service, 'Background to Oil', November 1979

Table 1.4 The major recipients of oil exports from the Persian Gulf, 1984–6 (thousand tonnes)

	Total oil imports			% from the Gulf			Imported from Iran			Imported from Iraq		
	1984	1985	1986	1984	1985	1986	1984	1985	1986	1984	1985	1986
USA	171,847 (22,396)	160,699 (12,045)	206,148 (39,564)	13	7	19	507	1,356	800	611	2,266	3,945
West Germany	66,934 (11,071)	64,194 (6,768)	66,569 (10,112)	17	11	15	2,422	2,667	2,037	1,988	330	733
France	69,946 (21,532)	68,657 (21,038)	65,998 (25,662)	31	31	39	3,399	4,076	2,924	3,126	6,430	4,835
Italy	66,358 (25,246)	63,434 (19,357)	71,908 (31,475)	38	31	44	9,306	7,254	6,740	3,554	4,669	4,019
Netherlands	43,950 (14,681)	37,791 (12,976)	46,098 (20,121)	33	34	44	8,450	4,438	3,326	1,038	1,290	3,019
Japan	183,065 (116,946)	168,825 (103,811)	164,987 (99,603)	64	61	61	12,879	12,294	11,050	712	3,504	7,962

Note: * Author's calculation.
  ( ) Figures in brackets represents the total oil imports from the Persian Gulf.
  (–) None.
Source: Statistiques 1986

Table 1.4 (continued)

	Kuwait			Qatar			Imported from UAE			Saudi Arabia		
	1984	1985	1986	1984	1985	1986	1984	1985	1986	1984	1985	1986
USA	1,213	1,823	1,400	204	–	520	4,419	1,680	1,817	15,442	6,561	31,082
West Germany	258	136	7	737	496	–	1,118	262	81	4,548	2,877	7,254
France	128	551	439	2,174	1,645	1,287	4,195	2,369	1,526	8,510	5,967	14,651
Italy	117	1,472	3,143	859	320	300	2,457	870	2,323	8,953	4,772	14,950
Netherlands	2,994	2,899	3,538	769	356	323	78	812	110	1,358	3,181	9,805
Japan	6,925	7,764	10,307	10,652	9,601	7,872	27,549	35,543	35,284	55,529	35,105	27,128

This observation on the paramount global economic significance of the Gulf makes the relative neglect of the coverage of the economic consequences of the war even more striking.

It is therefore expected that my study will contribute in some measure to a better understanding of the Gulf War and will fill the gap which currently exists in the coverage of the economic consequences of the conflict.

The major consequences of the war in general are:

destruction of wealth. There has been a massive loss of both human and non-human capital, leading to a large reduction in productivity, and loss of foreign-exchange earnings.

Sacrifice of potential output, owing to the transfer of the labour force from a peace-time economy to a military and war-related economy. Therefore resources are not allocated to their most efficient uses or to their most efficient locations, thus resulting in increased costs and reductions in efficiency.

a brain-drain and outgoing of human capital leading to a smaller skilled and semi-skilled labour force.

a reduction in the quality of human capital resulting from an unprecedented call-up to military service of students in schools, high schools and universities, and from the flight of the academics and professional classes to Western countries.

a rise in domestic inflation, arising from more expensive imports, an increase in black-market trading, and an increase in commercial activities (i.e. importing and its distribution) at the expense of domestic production.

crippling of the agricultural sector, leading to massive shortfalls in production, thus resulting in a serious state of dependency on the outside world for food supplies.

a huge rise in military expenditure (Milex), leading to an increased defence burden.

a massive increase in defence-related imports, leading to an increased arms-imports burden, with much negative impact on the economy as a whole.

the failure to diversity exports and thus the tendency to become increasingly more dependent on the oil sector to provide the much needed foreign-exchange earnings.

in the case of Iraq, the loss of its $35 billion foreign-exchange reserves (at the start of the war) and the creation of a huge international indebtedness.

This book, describing the economic consequences of the Iran–Iraq war, is an attempt to shed light on the above points, amongst others.

The war

This study is not of why nations go to war,[4] but none the less it would be beneficial if at this stage we shed some light on the background to, and some of the apparent reasons for, the Iran–Iraq war.

By the mid-1970s Iran had become the absolute and undisputed power in the Gulf. This, for example, was acknowledged in 1975, when Iraq, formally accepted Iran's military superiority by signing the Algiers Agreement, which provided for the following:

1 Demarcation of the land frontier in accordance with the 1913 Protocol of Constantinople and the verbal accord of 1914.
2 Agreement to demarcate the Shatt al-Arab waterway on the basis of the *thalweg* (i.e. deep-water line).
3 Agreement to restore security and mutual confidence along their common boundaries, and to exercise a 'strict and effective control' with the aim of finally putting an end to 'all acts of infiltration of a subversive character' from either side.
4 The pledge of both parties to regard the provisions negotiated at the 1975 OPEC [Organization of Petroleum Exporting Countries] meeting as indivisible elements of a comprehensive settlement, such that a breach of any one would be considered a violation of the spirit of the Algiers Agreement.[5]

Given the above, as Karsh (1987) has noted, there is little doubt as to which party to the agreement made the most concessions. Whereas Iraq went a long way to acknowledge Iran's sovereignty over half of the Shatt al-Arab waterway, Iran in practice made no concession. There is no doubt that to sign this agreement was a humiliating experience for Sadam Hussain.

However, this agreement, leading to the Pax Irana of the 1975–9 period, opened a new era in Iran–Iraq relations. The former *status quo* arrangements based on the 1937 Agreement,[6] were replaced by a relationship that assumed unquestioned Iranian superiority and dominance in the Gulf. Given this, Iran under the Shah, now more aggressively than ever before, carried on with its 'big-push' strategy of development, both in the civilian and military sectors.

On the other hand, Iraq became much more 'inward' looking, focusing on the build-up of its infrastructure and improving its defences which had been considerably destabilized as a result of the Kurdish conflict which had been supported by Iran until the Algiers Agreement was signed. Moreover, it should be noted that, in contrast to Iran, Iraq adopted during this period a 'less-big' strategy of development which in the end proved to be a much better and wiser policy.

The origins of the war

Many theories and points of view have been put forward to explain the Iran–Iraq war and its causes, ranging from centuries-old religious (Sunni vs. Shia) and ethnic (Arab vs. Persian) differences and disputes between the two people to personal animosity between Iraq's President Hussain and Iran's Ayatollah Khomeini.[7]

A further model, based on the grand-design theory, identifies the main cause of the war as the Iraqi leader's personal ambitions. These range from the occupation of Iranian territories to the overthrow of the new revolutionary regime, which would remove the threat of the spread of Islamic fundamentalism and thus make Iraq the pre-eminent Arab and Gulf State, as well as the leading force within the Non-Aligned Movement (see, for example, Cordesman 1984 and Standenmaier 1983).

Another study rejects the above analysis and puts forward the point of view that the Iraqi invasion of Iran did not emanate from a premeditated grand design but was a pre-emptive move, intended to forestall the Iranian threat to the existence of the Ba'ath regime (Karsh 1988).

However, as far as the present author is concerned, I would like to say that there exists some truth in all the above-mentioned theories, and together they provide a 'good' explanation of the main causes of the Iran–Iraq war.

None the less it should be said that, by the time the Shah had fallen and was replaced by a totally and diametrically different regime, the war between the two countries had become inevitable. Iran was now a theocracy and traditionalist, while Iraq was secular and modernist. The two states now had unquestionably different views and objectives, domestically, regionally and internationally, views that, unlike the situation during the Shah's period, could not have been reconciled. Indeed, the duration of the war goes a long way to establish this point.

Given the above, as well as the vacuum caused by the Shah's fall, a 'time bomb' condition was created which had to explode, and it did on 22 September 1980.

In order to note why the 'explosion' happened so soon after the revolution, one has to know what Iran and Iraq were like on the eve of the war. Therefore, at this point the pre-war military and economic balances of the two countries will be noted.

The military balance on the eve of war

If we look at the situation from a purely military point of view, it can be said that the timing of the Iraqi invasion could not have been better chosen. At the time of the Shah's overthrow, the Iranian armed forces were thrown into total disarray. They were regarded as the Shah's instrument of oppression, and also as the most serious potential source of counter-revolution, so the new revolutionary regime was quick to reduce the armed forces' capabilities even further by systematic purges.[8]

It has been noted that, by the outbreak of the war, some 85 senior officers had been executed and hundreds more (including all major-generals and most of the brigadier generals) were imprisoned or forced to retire. In all, by the time of the war, some 12,000 high-ranking officers had been purged, 10,000 of them from the army (Hickman 1982). Moreover, the armed forces were affected further by their inability to enlist new recruits, as well as the mass desertion in the early stages of the revolution.

Furthermore, the purges and their consequences, as well as the attempts by the revolutionary regime to establish the Revolutionary Guard Corps, the *Pasdaran,* meant that, by the time of the invasion, Iran had no Joint Staff to co-ordinate the war strategy through a central command-and-control system (Karsh 1987). It is also noted that the US advisers on their departure from Iran had erased the data on the computer-based inventory-control system for spare parts, thus making it almost impossible for Iranian military personnel to locate and identify the mass of spares in depots (Karsh 1987).

If Iran's armed forces were in disarray and in a state of humiliation, Iraq's forces were in a jubilant mood. The strength of the army which had brought disgrace upon them by forcing them to give in to the Shah's demands in Algiers had now diminished. By September 1980 Iraq, maybe for the first time, found itself militarily in a position where the balance of power had tipped in its favour (Karsh 1987). So it seems that, based on what was happening in Iran, Saddam Hussain made a calculation and then ordered his forces to invade the old-enemy's territory.

The economic balance on the eve of war (with special reference to the oil sector and oil revenues)

For about two years or so prior to the war, Iran's economy had been in turmoil. As the revolution was gathering momentum, so were the strikes and riots which by the end of 1978 had brought the country to a standstill. By December 1978 there was a complete cessation of oil exports. In March 1979, under the new revolutionary regime, the oil exports were resumed, but at a lower level than before the revolution. Oil production in April–June 1979 was 3.9 million barrels per day (mbd) as compared with 5.7 mbd in 1977 and the first nine months of 1978. The corresponding figures for oil exports during the same period were 3.5 mbd and 5 mbd (for evidence on these figures see BP 1981 and *Petroleum Economist*, various issues).

Furthermore, even the lower rate of production was not being maintained. For example, three months prior to the war, i.e. June–August 1980, production averaged 1.4 mbd, while oil exports had dropped to about 1 mbd, compared to 2.4 mbd in 1979. (BP 1981 and *Petroleum Economist,* various issues.)

The sharp rise in oil prices preceding the Iranian revolution had mostly offset the reduction in oil exports and thus Iran's oil revenues did not decline so drastically. Nevertheless the rapid decline in oil production and exports depressed the revenues to about $19.2 billion in 1979, from $23.6 billion in 1977 and $21.7 billion in 1978.

As far as Iraq is concerned, its situation was in total contrast to Iran's. Iraq's economy was booming during the late 1970s. Oil output had increased from 2 mbd in 1973 to 2.7 mbd in 1978, rising by 30 per cent to 3.5 mbd in 1979. Oil revenues had also risen significantly from $1.8 billion in 1973 to $10.8 billion in 1978. By 1979 the oil revenues had risen by 97.2 per cent to $21.3 billion (for evidence on these figures see Statistiques 1978–81). In the first nine months of 1980, oil-export revenues were $22.4 billion, or about $29.8 billion on an annual basis (had the war not started on 22 September 1980, and if we assume a constant rate of production/export for the remainder of the year).

In all, as far as the economy is concerned, Iran was in turmoil, with reduced oil production/exports and revenues, while Iraq was in a situation of 'never had it so good', with years of sustained economic growth, the build-up of its infrastructure, a rapid and unparalleled rise in oil production/exports and revenues. The difference between the two countries' oil exports, before and since the invasion, can best be observed in figure 1.1.

In sum, on the eve of the war, Iran and Iraq, economically speaking, could not have been more different and further apart than they were.

The foregoing is a bird's-eye view of aspects of the Iran–Iraq war in so far as it relates to the origin, causes, and the military/economic conditions of both countries on the eve of the invasion.

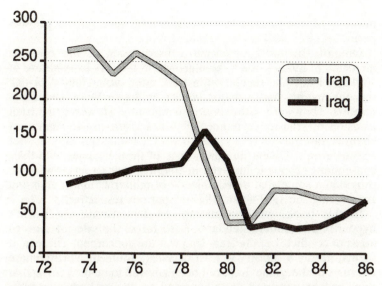

Figure 1.1 Oil exports by Iran and Iraq, 1973–86 (million tonnes)
Sources: Mofid 1987: 150–1, table 4.3; *Statistiques* 1974–86; UN
Department of International and Economic Affairs (1979–83) *Yearbook
of World Energy Statistics*; OECD 1974–86; 1986, No. 1; BP (1986).

It can be seen that, from a purely military and economic point of
view, the timing of the Iraqi invasion of Iran apparently could not
have been chosen more wisely. In the months prior to the
offensive, Iraq for the first time found itself in a position to deliver
the final and fatal blow against Iran.

Regardless of why nations go to war, which could be argued
under different theories and models, there is a real tangible and
measurable consequence of the war; that is, the impact of the war
on the economy, which is the main objective of this book.

An overview of the book

The analysis of the economic consequen es of the war on Iran's
and Iraq's economies, as well as the economic consequences of the
rapid militarization of the Gulf countries are the principal focus of
this book. Chapters two and three therefore provide a study of the
impact of the conflict on some aspects of the Iranian and the Iraqi
economies. These two chapters will emphasize oil production/
exports; foreign-exchange earnings; non-defence foreign trade and
the performance of the agricultural sector since the war. For the

purpose of comparison the corresponding data on the pre-war period of 1973–9/80 is also provided.

One of the most significant consequences of the oil-price increases of 1973–4 was a rapid growth in military expenditure of Iran and Iraq. The revolution in Iran, after successfully deposing the old regime, had a major impact on Iran's Milex and arms-imports. They were both reduced significantly. However, the Iraqi invasion of Iran in September 1980 has given rise to significant changes, not only on Iran's pattern of Milex and arms-imports, but also on Iraq's. Given the significance of these changes, and their consequent economic impacts, in chapters four to seven we have provided a somewhat detailed study of militarization of Iran and Iraq during the 1973–8 and 1979–85 periods respectively.

In this book, we also attempt to demonstrate the world's hypocrisy and double standards in so far as the sales of arms to areas of conflict, i.e. the Iran–Iraq war are concerned. There is, it seems, hardly a country in East or West, South or North, where the rules of the 'game' have not been allowed to be broken, so that arms can be exported or re-exported to one or both countries. Chapter eight therefore will look at the Gulf War and the international arms trade.

The revolution in Iran and the rise of Shi'ite fundamentalism in largely Sunni-Muslim-dominated countries in the Persian Gulf were among the main reasons for a rapid increase in military expenditure and arms imports in the Gulf countries in the late 1970s. It is important to note that such rapid increases in Milex have taken place at a time when oil revenues have been falling and thus resources have become more scarce. Now, more than ever before, the oil-exporting economies of the Gulf face a serious 'butter vs. guns' dilemma. To shed light on these issues, in chapter nine we shall look at the impact of the war on Milex and the arms imports of Saudi Arabia and Kuwait.

In chapter ten we shall attempt to bring together the various component parts of the economic cost of the war to Iran and Iraq and to assign a dollar value to the war's costs. Chapter eleven, the conclusion to the book, summarizes the conclusions to the previous chapters and then tries to put forward some recommendations concerning the eventual post-war reconstruction of Iran and Iraq.

Since major parts of this study cover topics such as foreign-exchange earnings, foreign trade, agricultural production and imports, military expenditure and arms imports, etc., it was deemed necessary to provide the data and analysis supporting the arguments presented. These include the tables, graphs, charts, notes and appendices. For those less inclined to go though the mass of detail, brief summary chapters are included.

Chapter two

Iran and Iraq at war: the analysis of the economic consequences

Introduction

On 16 January 1979 the Shah's 37-year rule came to an end, when he left Iran never to return, a price that it seems he had to pay for his misguided and unacceptable policies, both in the civilian and defence sectors in Iran (for further reading on these issues see Mofid 1987).

On 1 February of the same year, Ayatollah Khomeini returned to Iran and was greeted by millions. In April Iran became an Islamic Republic. According to the revolutionary leaders, as a result of the Shah's policies, Iran had become too dependent on oil revenues and had failed to diversify its exports.

Moreover, it was argued that (demonstrated in Mofid 1987) much of these revenues was being spent on imports of lavish consumer goods and military-related hardware. It was also contended that Iran under the Shah had become too dependent on the West for its imports. Furthermore it was also argued that the Shah's policies had resulted in the destruction of the agricultural sector, pushing Iran into a serious state of dependency on imported food. The revolution, it was claimed, would reduce Iran's military expenditures and arms imports, would expand the agricultural sector, make Iran self-sufficient in food, diversify and increase Iran's non-oil exports, reduce imports, especially consumer-goods imports, and finally reduce Iran's reliance on the West (Mofid 1987).

However, little did they (the revolutionary leaders) know that, while the revolution was still very young, Iran was going to be invaded and that there would be serious consequences for the projected goals and objectives of the revolution.

Given this, we shall now attempt to provide a study of the economic consequences of the war on Iran and Iraq, with special reference to oil production/exports, foreign-exchange earnings, non-defence foreign trade and agricultural performance since the war. For the purpose of comparison, throughout this chapter, the corresponding data for the pre-Revolution/war period of 1973–8/ 79 is also provided. The changes during these two periods will then be noted, and this in turn will present some of the economic consequences of the war on both countries. This will be done by an analysis of the effects of the war on each country separately, starting with Iran in this chapter, to be followed by Iraq in the following chapter.

The economic consequences of the war for Iran

In order to assess the economic consequences of the war for Iran, it would be most beneficial if, at this point, some of the objectives of the Islamic Republic with regard to their goals of planning, as illustrated in the First Five-Year Economic, Social and Cultural Development Plan, are noted. These observations show, what Iran would have been like (a) if there had been no war and (b) if the Islamic Republic had been successful in achieving its objectives.

Some of the main objectives and priorities of the Plan are as follows:

securing economic independence.
provision of food and clothing.
provision of housing.
elimination of unemployment.
prevention of consumerism.
agriculture as the axis of development.
expansion of non-oil exports.
preventing the expansion of large cities and implementing settlement policies (Mofid 1987: 206).

As far as foreign-trade orientations are concerned, the Plan had projected 97 per cent and 3 per cent shares of oil and non-oil exports in total exports for 1983, with the latter's share rising to 7.1 per cent in 1987 (Mofid 1987: 26, table 7.2).

As for the imports, the Plan's major objective was to decrease Iran's dependency on the outside world by reducing the share of consumer-goods imports in total imports, from 22.3 per cent in 1983 to 14.2 per cent in 1987 (Mofid 1987).

Therefore, when analysing the impact of the war on Iran's economy, not only should we compare and contrast the pre- and post-war changes, but also note the outcome of the Plan objectives. It is then that we can have a clearer picture of the consequences of the war.

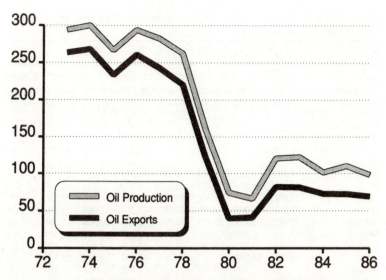

Figure 2.1 Oil production and exports: Iran, 1973–86 (million tonnes)
Sources: Mofid 1987: 150–1, table 4.3; *Statistiques* 1979–85; UN
Department of International and Social Affairs (1979–81) *Yearbook of
World Energy Statistics*; OECD 1984; 1986, No. 1; BP 1986.

The impact of the war on oil production and exports

The volume of oil production and exports has been subjected to
much imbalance since the revolution and the start of the war. The
figures for oil production and exports during the 1973–85 period
are provided in table 2.1, and their graphical presentation is
illustrated in figure 2.1. As can be seen, oil production decreased
by 54 and 11 per cent between 1979/80 and 1980/1, where it
declined from 159,496 thousand tonnes in 1979 to only 66,252
thousand tonnes in 1981. By 1982 the situation had improved
considerably, oil production had increased by 82 per cent to
120,396 thousand tonnes. From then onwards oil production
declined and, by 1985, it had fallen to 110,100 thousand tonnes.
The corresponding figure for 1986 is 94,100 thousand tonnes
(Statistiques 1986).

In all, on average each year, oil production has declined by 7.2
per cent during the 1979–86 period. The corresponding figure for
the pre-Revolution/war period of 1973 to 1978 was a decline of 2.2
per cent on average each year.

Given the imbalance in oil production, there has also been an
imbalance in oil exports. The export of oil fell by 67 per cent from

Table 2.1 Oil production and major recipients of Iran's oil exports, 1973–85 (thousand tonnes)

Year	1973	1974	1975	1976	1977	1978	1979	1980
Oil production	293,908	299,949	266,676	293,951	282,224	262,436	159,496	74,077
Oil export	263,443	268,207	233,406	260,685	242,891	220,436	121,187	40,112
Destination:								
USA	12,496	21,655	13,693	28,230	39,790	43,061	27,733	1,077
Canada	5,172	6,209	9,300	7,861	6,056	5,137	2,274	65
West Germany	3,500	4,785	14,190	19,290	15,770	17,289	11,540	5,735
UK	48,512	46,831	20,423	22,713	14,193	11,895	5,069	1,249
Italy	12,691	6,509	12,860	14,530	14,410	14,335	2,224	952
France	10,514	11,005	13,290	14,550	9,385	10,904	6,130	1,228
Netherlands	19,925	32,839	17,415	17,690	13,525	20,559	5,284	644
Belgium	7,221	4,685	5,358	5,338	7,296	7,478	2,685	1,066
Spain	5,384	3,275	4,506	11,854	11,043	8,600	4,379	3,152
Japan	84,580	66,752	55,677	46,168	40,570	38,860	23,659	13,443
Australia	500	300	1,033	854	901	359	134	50
Turkey	374	867	113	1,674	1,740	4,970	1,100	2,771
Others (including Eastern bloc)*	52,116	62,495	65,446	69,938	68,212	36,989	26,966	8,121

Note: * Author's calculation: all the percentages have been rounded up and therefore totals may not add up to 100.
Sources: Mofid 1987: 150–1, table 4.3. *Statistiques*, 1979 to 1985, BP *Statistical Review of World Energy*, UN Department of International Economic and Social Affairs (1979–81) *Yearbook of World Energy Statistics* OECD 1984, 1986, No. 1., BP (1986) *Statistical Review of World Energy*, June

121,187 thousand tonnes in 1979 to only 40,112 thousand tonnes in 1980. It then rose significantly to 81,724 thousand tonnes in 1982. By 1985 oil exports had declined to 72,100 thousand tonnes and continued to fall to only 58,100 thousand tonnes in 1986 (Statistiques 1986).

In all, during the 1979/86 period, oil exports have declined by an annual average of 10 per cent, while, during the 1973–8 period, the corresponding figure was a decline of only 3.1 per cent.

Therefore it could be said that one of the major consequences of the war has been the decline in oil production and its exports; while every effort has been made to increase them.

With regard to the main recipients of oil exports, an important feature of table 2.1 is the fact that, in contrast to the many statements made by the officials, that 'the Islamic Republic of Iran

Table 2.1 (continued)

Year	1981	1982	1983	1984	1985						
Oil production	66,252	120,396	122,150	101,400	110,100	*% share of total exports**					
Oil export	41,079	81,724	81,100	72,600	72,100	*1973*	*1977*	*1978*	*1979*	*1983*	*1985*
Destination:											
USA	3,388	2,608	5,028	2,896	3,412	4.9	16.4	19.5	22.8	6.2	4.4
Canada	–	465	2,189	417	533	1.9	2.5	2.3	1.8	2.7	0.7
West Germany	1,504	2,311	2,067	2,423	2,666	1.3	6.5	7.8	9.5	2.5	3.4
UK	1,284	2,578	749	2,773	623	18.4	5.8	5.3	4.1	0.9	0.8
Italy	2,800	13,116	11,854	9,496	7,292	4.8	5.9	6.5	1.8	14.6	9.4
France	1,520	3,761	4,248	3,395	4,077	3.9	3.9	4.9	5.0	5.2	5.3
Netherlands	473	7,220	6,855	7,653	4,381	7.5	5.6	9.3	4.3	8.4	5.6
Belgium	1,494	1,198	950	808	1,413	2.7	3.0	3.3	2.2	1,2	1.8
Spain	5,085	6,339	7,449	5,883	4,246	2.0	4.5	3.9	3.6	9.9	5.5
Japan	6,820	11,595	19,587	12,805	12,894	32.1	16.7	17.6	19.5	24.1	16.6
Australia	–	493	–	–	54	0.1	0.4	0.1	0.1	–	0.1
Turkey	1,485	3,168	5,376	7,453	5,448	0.1	0.7	2.2	0.9	6.6	7.0
Others (including Eastern bloc)*	15,266	26,114	14,748	16,598	30,418	17.9	26.2	14.7	22.2	18.2	39.3

would never sell oil to America' (BBC 1982), Iran has been selling oil to that country. Although exports of oil to the US have been much reduced in volume since the revolution, none the less, by 1985, 4.4 per cent of Iran's total oil exports were destined for the USA. In 1986, this share had increased to 7.8 per cent of the total as, in that year, the US had imported 4,541 thousand tonnes of oil from Iran (OECD 1987: third quarter).

France is another interesting case. While France, as a major supplier of arms to Iraq, has indirectly been responsible for so much death and destruction in Iran, none the less Iran has continued to sell oil to that country. In fact, during the 1979–85 period, on average each year France, like the US, has imported 4.5 per cent of Iran's total oil exports. By 1986 this share had increased to 5.6 per cent of the total, as in that year France imported 3,425 thousand tonnes of oil from Iran (OECD 1987: third quarter).

In all, while in 1979, Western Europe and Japan together had accounted for 50 per cent of Iran's total oil exports, by 1985 this share had changed to 58 per cent of the total, rising to 63 per cent in 1986 (OECD 1987: third quarter). Moreover, if we compare these figures with those of the pre-revolution (1973–8) period, it can be noted that, except for Italy, Spain and Turkey, the rest of the countries mentioned have reduced their overall imports of Iranian oil (i.e. they have reduced their overall dependency on Iran).

Another important feature of table 2.1 is the emergence of Turkey as one of the main importers of crude oil from Iran. While in 1979 less than 1 per cent of Iran's total oil exports were destined for Turkey, by 1985 this share had increased substantially to 7 per cent of the total oil exports. In 1986 Turkey imported 6,613 thousand tonnes of oil from Iran, representing 11.4 per cent of Iran's total oil exports in that year (OECD 1987: third quarter).

The importance of oil in providing foreign-exchange earnings during the period under study and the failure of the Islamic Republic to diversify Iran's foreign-exchange earnings can best be seen in table 2.2, where the value of Iran's total exports and its composition during the 1973–86 period are given. As can be noted, in 1979 crude petroleum had provided 87.2 per cent of the total value of exports. By 1986, however, this share had increased to 94 per cent.

The share of non-energy merchandise exports has corresponding- ingly fallen from the high level of 5.6 per cent in 1980 to 3.5 per cent in 1986. One reason for this is the jump in oil prices in 1979– 80 (OPEC II). The absolute decline of non-energy exports, however, indicates that the government's intentions are very far from being realized, even if price changes are allowed for. Furthermore the failure to diversify the sources of foreign- exchange earnings is also in contrast to the objectives of the First National Plan of the Islamic Republic.

If we compare and contrast the figures for the post- and pre- revolution periods, it can be noted that indeed, since the revolution, Iran has become much more dependent on oil revenues. During the 1973–8 period such revenues on average per year had provided 91.5 per cent of the total value of exports, while during 1982–6 this has increased to 98 per cent per annum.

Table 2.2 Value of Iran's total exports 1973–86 (billion current rials)

	1973	1974	1975	1976	1977	1978	1979	1980	1981	1982	1983	1984	1985	1986
TX	426	1,459	1,367	1,652	1,713	1,558	1,408	994	981	1,632	1,685	1,128	1,219	840[e]
Petroleum	387	1,414	1,328	1,610	1,667	1,528	1,352	938	944	1,608	1,660	1,103	1,194	810
CPX	365	1,336	1,245	1,539	1,539	1,470	1,228	684	731	1,508	1,621	1,066	1,157	790
N-EX*	39	45	39	42	46	30	56	56	37	24	25	25	25	30[e]
	%	%	%	%	%	%	%	%	%	%	%	%	%	%
Share of petroleum in TX*	90.8	96.7	97.1	97.4	97.3	98.1	96.0	94.4	96.2	98.2	98.6	97.8	98.0	96.4
Share of CPX in TX*	85.7	91.7	91.1	93.1	93.0	94.3	87.2	68.8	75.5	92.4	96.2	94.5	94.9	94.0
Share of N-EX in TX*	9.1	3.1	2.8	2.5	2.7	1.9	4.0	5.6	3.7	1.5	1.5	2.2	2.0	3.5

Notes: * Author's calculation.
TX Total exports.
CPX Crude petroleum exports.
N-EX Non-energy exports.
The exchange rate for the period under observation: $1 = rials 68.9 (1973), 67.6 (1974), 67.6 (1975), 70.2 (1976), 70.5 (1978), 70.5 (1979), 70.6 (1980), 78.3 (1981), 83.6 (1982), 86.4 (1983), 90.0 (1984), 91.0 (1985), 79.0 (1986).
[e] Author's estimation.

Sources: IMFa *International Financial Statistics* 1986, 1987
Statistiques 1986

The impact of the war on the value, composition and the origins of non-defence imports

As was noted already, the revolution had much criticized the Shah's foreign-trade performance and had made many promises to reverse these policies. Therefore an area in which we could clearly observe the impact of the war should be in the foreign-trade sector where much emphasis has been laid on achieving the objectives of the revolution.

It would be beneficial at this point if, once more, the main foreign-trade objectives of the revolution are noted. They are to reduce Iran's dependency on the West; to reduce the share of consumer goods in total imports; and to increase the share of non-oil exports in total exports (on these issues see further Mofid 1987: chapter seven). With these in mind, the value and the origins of Iran's non-military imports are the subject of the study at this point.

Table 2.3 provides data on the money value of total non-military imports during 1973 to 1985. It can be seen that the value of imports during the period under study has been the subject of much fluctuation. This is due to the fact that the value of imports is closely related to the value of foreign-exchange earnings (i.e. the amount of oil exports and oil prices). Thus an imbalance in oil revenues has also caused an imbalance in the value of imports.

As can be noted, total non-defence imports were $9,695 million in 1979, and rising to $11,630 million in 1982. However, by 1982/3, foreign-exchange earnings had improved significantly (see table 2.2). Given the close relationship between this and the imports, by 1983 the value of imports had increased also significantly to $18,227 million.

However, since 1983, as a result of sustained Iraqi attacks on Iran's oil facilities, as well as a decline in oil prices in general, there has been a rapid decline in foreign-exchange earnings and thus the value of imports has fallen sharply. In 1984 total imports fell to $14,750 million and still further to $11,658 in 1985. By 1986 total imports had fallen to only $9,775 million (IMFb 1986).

In all, total non-military imports have increased by only 0.1 per cent on average each year between 1979 and 1986. However, if we compare the 1986 imports with those of the 1983 period (the highest level since the revolution and the war), it can be noted that the total imports during this period have fallen by 18.7 per cent on average each year.

Such a decline in imports and the fact that Iran's industrialization has been based on 'dependent capitalism' and the import-substitution

Table 2.3 Value and distribution of Iran's imports by main countries: 1973–85 (million current dollars)*

	1973	1974	1975	1976	1977	1978	1979	1980	1981	1982	1983	1984	1985
USA	477	1,313	2,316	1,974	2,347	1,508	1,181	25	330	134	209	178	81
Canada	23	56	84	103	121	57	21	30	21	161	182	120	53
West Germany	717	1,178	2,033	2,273	2,789	2,142	1,413	1,657	1,766	1,536	3,310	2,518	1,812
UK	342	508	989	890	1,028	843	542	1,006	811	635	1,047	1,030	745
Italy	137	197	418	735	810	596	455	632	829	796	994	1,039	672
France	176	241	519	715	661	508	468	793	735	367	408	201	176
Netherlands	88	152	332	443	489	215	261	386	430	298	470	417	298
Belgium	112	172	291	279	348	257	175	297	281	160	270	253	195
Switzerland	71	115	188	227	271	275	245	304	260	211	336	311	219
Sweden	52	79	151	140	192	145	75	207	215	226	464	522	210
Spain	28	35	126	109	140	259	121	327	337	328	452	327	312
Japan	537	993	1,853	2,200	2,321	1,757	1,013	1,697	1,629	1,033	3,102	1,862	1,496
Australia	51	67	191	172	228	151	146	311	220	219	258	411	235
Turkey	15	38	55	41	40	23	21	93	257	811	978	969	661
India	54	113	435	315	193	94	118	144	158	150	129	132	110
Brazil	52	24	59	66	69	68	79	263	214	231	385	328	234
Others (including Soviet Union & Eastern Europe)	727	1,262	1,546	1,824	2,400	1,474	3,482	2,235	4,844	4,662	5,233	4,132	4,149
Total Imports	3,659	6,543	11,586	12,506	14,447	10,372	9,695	10,080	13,000	11,630	18,227	14,750	11,658

Note: * Excluding military-related imports.
Sources: Central Bank of Iran, *Annual Report and Balance Sheet*, 1356, 1358
IMFb 1981, 1985, 1986; IMFa *International Financial Statistics*, August 1985, December 1985 and November 1986
Mofid 1987: 154, 155, table 4.5

strategy of development (see further Mofid 1987: chapters three and four) with its massive import requirements, must have created many problems and setbacks in the economy. It should be underlined that, since the revolution, the import dependency of the economy has increased. For example, while in 1977 each 100 rials of non-oil gross domestic product (GDP) produced required 33 per cent of imported primary and intermediate inputs, by 1983 the corresponding figure had increased to 37 per cent (all figures based in constant rials, 1974 = 100) (for evidence on these figures see Behdad 1988: 10, table 4).

The serious state of import dependency of the 'large' (with ten or more workers) manufacturing establishments can further be seen in the fact that, according to the *Statistical Centre of Iran*, imported primary products accounted for 54 per cent of these establishments' total imports in 1983. For chemicals and basic metal industries, these shares were 69.7 and 71.5 per cent respectively in the same year (Statistical Centre of Iran 1985).

Given such a high dependency on imports, it would not be too difficult to note the effect of such imbalance and fluctuation in total imports on the performance of the industrial sector in Iran since the revolution and the war.

At this point, if the values of the pre- and post-war non-defence imports are compared, it can be noted that for example, during the 1973–7 period, they had increased by 41 per cent on average each year, while the corresponding figures for the 1981–6 and 1983–6 periods show a decline of 5.5 and 18.7 per cent respectively.

Table 2.4 provides figures for the share of non-military imports in GDP; that is, the measurement of import penetration during the 1973–86 period. As can be noted, the share of total non-military imports in GDP (including oil) on average per year during 1979 to 1986 is 10.1 per cent. The corresponding figure for the period 1979–83, to take account of the drastic fall in imports during 1984–6, is 11.9 per cent.

However, it should be noted that, in the first year of the revolution and the year preceding the Iraqi invasion, namely in 1979, although oil revenues were at the high level of 1,408 billion rials, the imports were kept at only 685 billion rials, representing an 11.3 per cent imports burden for that year, a much lower burden than the previous years, i.e. 19.6 per cent in 1977.

Therefore it appears that the revolutionary leaders were indeed genuine in their approach towards a new foreign-trade policy in Iran, and were serious in their initial actions to reduce Iran's import dependency. Thus the failure to achieve the objective of the revolution in this area can be said to be a serious consequence of the war.

Table 2.4 Iran's share of non-military imports in GDP* (oil inclusive and oil exclusive) 1973–86 (billion current rials)

	Total non-military imports	GDP (including oil)	Import ratio* GDP	GDP (excluding oil)	Import ratio* GDP
1973	248	1,784	14.0	1,196	21.0
1974	442	3,072	14.4	1,630	27.0
1975	782	3,479	22.5	2,103	37.0
1976	875	4,480	19.5	2,802	31.0
1977	1,022	5,207	19.6	3,545	29.0
1978	721	4,917	14.7	3,692	20.0
1979	685	6,053	11.3	4,377	15.7
1980	863	6,759	12.8	5,778	14.9
1981	985	8,218	12.0	7,288	13.5
1982	1,185	10,621	11.6	8,852	13.4
1983	1,528	13,471	11.7	11,662	13.6
1984	1,328	15,030	8.8	12,926e	10.3
1985	1,061	15,306	6.9	13,163e	8.1
1986	772	15,509	5.0	13,183e	6.0

Notes: * Author's calculation.
e Author's estimation.
Sources: Central Bank of Iran, *Annual Report and Balance Sheet*, 1351, 1356, 1357–82; IMFa (1980, 1987) *International Financial Statistics*

Table 2.5 Commodity composition of Iran's imports (non-military) classified by their use, 1973–86 (%)*

	1973	1974	1975	1976	1977	1978	1979	1980	1981	1982	1983	1984+	1985+	1986+
Intermediate goods (a)	60.3	65.2	53.2	52.5	53.9	51.5	54.6	57.2	60.0	57.9	59.5	55.5	54.0	52.0
Capital goods (b)	24.8	20.3	29.8	9.8	26.5	28.0	18.9	16.0	15.8	19.5	23.9	20.1	19.5	20.0
Consumer goods (c)	14.9	15.5	17.0	17.7	19.6	20.5	26.2	26.3	23.8	22.6	16.6	24.4	26.5	28.0
Total	100.0	100.0	100.0	100.0	100.0	100.0	100.0	100.0	100.0	100.0	100.0	100.0	100.0	100.0

Average share/Year (a) 1979–86*   56.9
Average share/Year (b) 1979–86*   19.1
Average share/Year (c) 1979–86*   24.0

Average share/Year (a)* 1973–8   56.1
Average share/Year (b)* 1973–8   26.5
Average share/Year (c)* 1973–8   17.6

Notes: * Author's calculation.
+ Author's estimation.
All figures rounded up, totals may not add up to 100.
Sources: Central Bank of Iran, *Annual Report and Balance Sheet*, 1356, 1358, 1361, 1362
Mofid 1987: 164, table 4.10

The composition of Iran's non-defence imports (percentage share in total) during the 1973–86 period is given in table 2.5. The import substitution (I-S) strategy of development and the goal of self-sufficiency since the revolution have meant that a large proportion of imports has been intermediate and capital-goods imports. Indeed, during the 1979–86 period, on average each year 56.9 and 19.1 per cent of total imports were intermediate and capital-goods imports.

At this point, if the figures of the pre- and post-revolution/war periods are compared, it can be observed that the share of intermediate goods imports has remained more or less unchanged; while the imports of capital goods on the other hand have declined significantly (see table 2.5).

The most significant change, given the revolution's goals and objectives, in particular to 'prevent consumerism', has been a substantial rise in imports of consumer goods. As shown in table 2.5, the import share of consumer goods, which during 1973–8 was 17.5 per cent of the total on average each year, has rapidly increased to 24 per cent on average per annum in the 1979–86 period.

In our analysis so far, we have used the current values of imports. We now analyse constant-price figures. The data on the value of total imports at 1974 constant prices has been calculated by using the index of industrial countries' export values, whose figures are given in table 2.6. As can be seen, the total non-military imports at 1974 constant prices was 434 billion rials in 1979, rising continuously and significantly to 983 billion rials in 1983.

Since 1983, however, given the rapid decline in oil revenues and consequently the fall in imports at current prices, there has also been a decline in imports at constant prices. They fell significantly to only 462 billion rials in 1986.

In all, during 1979 to 1986, the imports at 1974 constant prices have increased by 0.9 per cent on average each year. The corresponding figure for the 1979–83 period, to take account of the drastic fall in imports during the 1984–6 period, is the rise of 22.7 per cent on average each year, while the figure for the 1983–6 period is the decline of 22.2 per cent on average each year. Total imports at 1974 constant prices during the pre-war period of 1973–8 had increased by 5.6 per cent on average each year.

What all these figures tell us is the existence of very chaotic and disorganized economic conditions in Iran, which in turn, have created a nightmare for planners and planning in general. One cannot plan the economy on a long-term basis when there are yearly fluctuations of these magnitudes in imports, given the

Table 2.6 Estimation of Iran's non-military imports at 1974 constant prices*, 1973–86 (billion constant rials)

	1973	1974	1975	1976	1977	1978	1979	1980	1981	1982	1983	1984	1985	1986
Total non-military imports (current prices)	248	442	782	875	1,022	721	686	863	985	1,185	1,583	1,328	1,061	772
Index of industrial countries' export values 1974 = 1	0.62	1.0	1.1	1.3	1.4	1.3	1.6	1.8	1.7	1.7	1.6	1.5	1.5	1.7
Total non-military imports at 1974 constant prices	400	442	711	673	730	555	434	482	573	714	983	862	689	462

Average annual growth of imports at 1974 constant prices (%)*

1973–8	5.6
1979–86	0.9
1983–6	−22.2

Note: * Author's calculations.
Sources: Central Bank of Iran *Annual Report and Balance Sheet*, 1356, 1359; IMFa (1980, 1985, 1987) *International Financial Statistics*

'dependent' capitalist nature of the economy. The war and the instability that it has caused have made a bad situation worse.

At this point the origins of Iran's imports since the revolution/ war, whose data was provided in table 2.3, is the subject of analysis. At the outset, it should be underlined that, since the revolution, the motivation of foreign-trade policy has been partly political, as, for example, the ban on trade with the US, and there has been a declared preference for trading with the Third World, as well as attempts to reduce the volume of trade with the West (see further Mofid 1987: chapter 7).

However, as it will be demonstrated shortly, the war and the desire to satisfy the immediate needs of the population, have made the achievement of the objectives of the revolution much more difficult, if not impossible.

By looking at table 2.3, it can be noted that the major pre-war suppliers, namely, West Germany and Japan, are still the main exporters to Iran. In 1979 they had accounted for 14.5 and 10.4 per cent of Iran's total imports. The corresponding figures for 1985 are 15.5 and 12.8 per cent.

In all, while in 1980 industrial countries had provided 66 per cent of total imports, by 1986 not much had been changed, as in that year their share was 65 per cent of the total. However, the European countries' share of the total, during the same period, has increased from 7 to 14 per cent. The share of African countries has remained unchanged, accounting for about 0.4 per cent of the total during the same period (IMF 1986b).

If we now compare the above figures with those of the pre-war period (i.e. 1979), it can be seen that the share of the industrialized countries in that year was 71 per cent of the total. Therefore, in comparison to 1986, since the war, there has been a modest decline (6 per cent) in Iran's total imports from these groups of countries. However, on the other hand, there has been a massive increase in the share of European countries, as their share in 1979 was only 3.4 per cent of the total; at the same time the African countries' share has also declined from 3.4 per cent of the total to only 0.4 per cent (IMF 1986b).

In conclusion, it can be said that, because of the fall in total Iranian oil exports, it is also true that Western European countries as well as Japan have substantially reduced their oil imports from Iran since the revolution. But, as was noted, Iran has not decreased its imports from these countries. Overall, although there has been some diversification of trading partners in post-revolution Iran, the changes have not been significant enough to reduce Iran's dependency on countries like West Germany and Japan, although,

Table 2.7 Iran's production of principal crop products, 1973–85 (thousand metric tonnes)*

Item	1973	1974	1975	1976	1977	1978	1979	1980	1981	1982	1983	1984	1985
Wheat	4,600	4,700	5,570	6,044	5,517	5,526	5,800	5,700	6,518	6,500	5,956	5,500	6,000
Rice	1,334	1,313	1,430	1,566	1,400	1,280	1,420	1,212	1,500	1,400	1,216	1,600	1,100
Barley	923	863	1,438	1,487	1,230	1,276	1,000	1,100	1,351	1,400	1,413	1,550	1,650
Corn	25	25	65	80	55	60	57	60	50	53	50	50	50
Sugar beet	4,940	4,200	4,670	5,250	4,150	3,653	3,900	1,500	2,318	2,100	3,650	3,290	3,385
Sugar cane	1,050	1,200	940	600	1,000	898	1,399	1,400	1,400	1,300	1,600	2,200	2,150
Cotton (raw)	615	715	470	510	535	472	278	180	211	294	202	226	200
Bovine meat	99	102	104	108	160	160	161	171	181	190	165	165	168
Mutton and lamb	158	152	167	171	176	224	230	232	225	225	230	234	234
Poultry	100	103	106	130	189	208	211	211	213	215	230	235	240
Cows' milk (fresh)	1,050	1,150	1,230	1,250	1,300	1,580	1,580	1,550	1,627	1,705	1,650	1,650	1,700
Sheep milk (fresh)	555	570	593	617	640	664	687	690	710	731	705	705	715
Cheese	77	81	85	86	89	98	98	99	102	105	104	104	106
Butter	48	51	54	56	58	66	66	67	69	72	70	70	71

Note: * Figures are rounded to the nearest 1,000 tonnes.
Sources: FAOa 1975, 1977, 1979, 1980, 1984, 1985

at the same time, these countries have reduced their dependency on Iranian oil.

The impact of the war on the agricultural sector

One of the most tragic consequences of the war, as we will demonstrate shortly, has been the failure of the agricultural sector to meet the basic requirements of the people. This has been the case, even though, as was mentioned earlier, the revolution had declared agriculture as the 'axis of development', had promised self-sufficiency in food and, in all, a total reversal of the policies discredited in the past. Therefore the following is an attempt to demonstrate what has been happening in the agricultural sector since the revolution and the war.

The figures for the estimated production of principal crop products and main livestock items during 1973–85 are given in table 2.7. It can be observed that the average annual growth rates for many items during the 1979–85 period have been either negative or increasing at a very insignificant rate. For example, the production of wheat during the period under study grew by 0.6 per cent on average each year; rice (−4 per cent); bovine meat (0.7 per cent); mutton and lamb (0.3 per cent); sheep milk (0.7 per cent) and cheese (1 per cent).

The above figures will prove more meaningful if they are compared with the rate at which the population has been growing during the same period. The population has increased from 37.2 million in 1979 to 44.2 million in 1985 (IMF 1986a), representing an average annual growth rate of 2.9 per cent. This observation very clearly demonstrates the failure of the agricultural sector to meet the food requirements of a growing population. The reasons for such an outcome are varied and complex. To elaborate on them is indeed beyond the scope of this study. However, there can be no doubt that the mounting costs of the war and the increased rural/urban migration caused by it are amongst the main reasons. The following is an attempt to clarify this observation.

Since the revolution there have been many attempts to increase the productivity of the agricultural sector by shifting the emphasis from industrial to agricultural development. Thus, for example, land under cultivation has increased significantly. Table 2.8 provides information on land use since the revolution. As can be noted, between 1979 and 1985, land under use for wheat production increased by 32.3 per cent; barley (47.4 per cent); sugar beet (10.3 per cent); cotton (31 per cent) and rice (58 per cent). However, given the significant increase in land under cultivation, then why, as was noted earlier, has agricultural production either declined or been static during the same period?

Table 2.8   Land under cultivation (thousand acres)

	1979	1980	1981	1982	1983	1984	1985	1979–85 % change
Wheat	11,705	12,940	15,202.5	15,480	15,105	14,897.5	15,485	32.3
Barley	3,535	4,152.5	3,597.5	4,602.5	5,015	5,407.5	5,210	47.4
Sugar Beet	328.5	353	422.5	457.5	420	335	362.5	10.3
Cotton	359.75	437.25	340	495	460	522.5	465	31.0
Rice	750.41	796.75	1,147.5	1,207.5	1,072.5	1,102.5	1,187.5	

Source: Ministry of Agriculture (1983, 1986) *Agricultural Economic Report*

Table 2.9   Sale and delivery of tractors, fertilizers (units and thousand tons)

	1982	1983	1984	1985	% change
Tractors	28,940	32,918	23,860	15,840	45.0 (1982–5)
Fertilizers	1,312	1,931	1,679	1,626	15.8 (1983–5)

Source: Ministry of Agriculture (1986) *Agricultural Economic Report*

The answer to this question is directly related to the consequences of the war. Why? Because, as a result of the war and its mounting costs, there has been less money available for necessary expenditures in the agricultural sector. For example, as shown in table 2.9, the number of tractors sold and delivered to the farmers declined by 45 per cent during the 1982–5 period, and the volume of fertilizers also declined by 15.8 per cent during the 1983–5 period, even though, as was noted already, there has been a significant rise in land use.

However, the government in Tehran had hoped that, by employing more people on the larger area of cultivated land, production could be increased, with greater reliance on traditional methods of production, rather than employing more capital-intensive techniques. Therefore, given this strategy, there was a need for a larger labour force to work on the land than ever before. However, the war very soon put an end to the realization of the said objective, as an increasing proportion of a young and able workforce from the rural areas was called up to go to the war front, while the remaining people either were too old to work on the land or chose to go to the larger cities themselves.

Since the war, many villages have been deserted altogether. For example, in Malayer, by 1983, 65 out of nearly 254 villages had been deserted (*Keyhan*: 20 July 1983). As far as internal migration is concerned, nation-wide data on rural–urban migration is scarce. Estimates, however, indicate that 40 per cent of the urban population growth between 1977 and 1983 has been due to peasant migration (Kazerooni 1985). According to official estimates, during 1979–83, 2.2 million people have moved from rural to urban areas, although independent studies estimate this figure to be at least three times higher (Kazerooni 1985). It is interesting to note that, according to another independent observer (Simpson 1988), the population of Tehran, for example, has increased from 6 million in 1978 to more than 10 million in 1986, representing an average annual increase of over 19 per cent during the same period.

The official information on the (percentage) share of the economically active population in agriculture in Iran for selected years between 1965 to 1985 is given in table 2.10. As a matter of interest, the corresponding figures for India, Pakistan and Turkey are also given.

By looking at table 2.10 and comparing the different sets of data, the scale of Iran's rural–urban migration, in absolute, as well as relative terms, becomes very clear. As can be seen, in 1965, 49 per cent of Iran's economically active population were in rural areas. By 1980 these figures had dropped to 36 per cent and the corresponding figure for 1985 is 33 per cent.

Table 2.10 Percentage share of economically active population in agriculture – a measurement of urbanization – Iran, India, Pakistan and Turkey (selected years)

	Iran	*India*	*Pakistan*	*Turkey*
1965	49	73	60	75
1970	44	72	59	71
1975	40	71	57	65
1980	36	70	55	58
1985	33	69	52	52

Source: FAOa 1985

One of the many reasons for the rapid urbanization in Iran, at least up to the revolution, was the misguided and inappropriate agricultural and industrial policies under the Shah, which have been addressed by the present author elsewhere already (Mofid 1987).

The revolution, however, had made the rural–urban migration a very important issue, and indeed the 'prevention of the expansion of large cities and implementing settlement policies' became one of the main objectives of planning in the post-revolution period. Given this, the failure of the Islamic Republic to stop or even to slow down the urbanization process is one of the most costly and tragic consequences of the war.

The failure to produce enough agricultural products has resulted in a significant increase in Iran's dependency on the outside world for food.

Table 2.11 provides figures on imports of principal agricultural products and main livestock items during 1973 to 1985. As can be seen, the imports of many items on average each year have increased significantly both before and since the revolution. But it should not be forgotten that the revolution had promised self-sufficiency in food and had declared agriculture as the 'axis of development'. All the planning and policy instruments, it seems at least at the beginning, were directed towards the achievement of this objective.

Therefore the failure to reverse past policies and at least reduce Iran's dependency on the outside world for food supplies, although all the intentions were there to do so, must be one of the major consequences of the war.

Conclusion

In this chapter we mainly analyzed some of the major economic consequences of the war on Iran during the 1980–5 period. However, as noted in chapter one, economically and militarily speaking, at the time of the invasion the two countries could not have been more different and further apart.

Iran's armed forces were disintegrated and demoralized, and the economy was in ruins, while Iraq was enjoying a major boom under a situation of 'never had it so good', so to say.

The chapter noted that the economic consequences of the war on Iran have been devastating. In a nutshell it can be seen that the most damaging consequence of the war on Iran has been the failure of the Islamic Republic to reverse the Shah's policies.

The revolution had promised to reduce Iran's dependency on oil revenues, diversify the economy, increase non-oil exports, reduce Iran's dependency on trade with the West, make agriculture the 'axis of development', increase food/agricultural production, reduce consumer-goods imports and finally put an end to the rural/urban migration.

In this chapter these issues were addressed and discussed and

Table 2.11 Iran's import of principal agricultural products, 1973–85 (thousand metric tonnes)*

	1973	1974	1975	1976	1977	1978	1979	1980	1981	1982	1983	1984	1985
Wheat and flour (wheat equivalent)	785	1,456	1,472	844	1,159	1,354	750	1,341	1,620	1,770	2,688	3,919	2,819
Rice	12	191	286	250	590	500	500	402	586	432	622	710	400
Barley	107	178	203	230	334	464	200	388	472	420	471	581	450
Corn	131	223	78	215	344	450	500	647	869	652	979	640	810
Sugar (total raw equivalent)	299	228	633	313	488	876	746	412	652	866	310	643	598
Sugar (refined)	161	98	424	220	449	732	686	379	600	674	285	592	550
Fresh/frozen bovine meat	4	5	15	22	40	28	42	60	46	53	119	85	50
Fresh/frozen sheep meat	12	19	38	58	60	50	59	110	124	162	114	145	130
Fresh/frozen poultry	3	2	17	22	18	21	28	64	65	40	43	42	10
Dry/fresh milk	7	11	14	11	19	28	29	21	47	41	53	25	20
Butter	16	21	27	26	28	26	45	38	66	43	67	59	52
Cheese	2	7	11	22	41	40	46	62	78	67	92	138	100

Note: * Figures are rounded to the nearest thousand tonnes.
Sources: FAOb 1975, 1977, 1979, 1982, 1983, 1985

the changes since the revolution/war were noted. We established that, in all cases, the situation has deteriorated and become more and more problematic.

The war therefore has had a most damaging and devastating effect on Iran's economic, industrial and agricultural development. Given that the revolution in Iran was a popular revolution, then the chances were that at least some, if not all, the objectives of the revolution could have been achieved by now.

Therefore the failure to realize any of the economic objectives of the revolution and to break from past economic policies can be identified as one of the most serious consequences of the war.

How successful the revolution would have been, in the absence of the war, in bringing about changes is a question beyond the ability of the present author to answer. However, let us not forget that the revolution was only seventeen months old when the country was invaded.

Chapter three

Iraq at war: the analysis of the economic consequences

Introduction

This chapter, which is a continuation of chapter two, provides a study of the impact of the war on some aspects of the Iraqi economy. As with the discussion of Iran, in this chapter we shall also emphasize oil production/exports; foreign exchange earnings; non-defence foreign trade and the performance of the agricultural sector since the war. As in chapter two, for the purpose of comparison, the corresponding data on the pre-war period of 1973–9 is also given. The changes during these two periods will then be noted, and this in turn will enable us to assess some of the economic consequences of the war on Iraq.

As noted in chapter one, Iraq's economy during the late 1970s was going through a period of unparalleled boom. Oil output had increased from 2.7 mbd in 1978 to 3.5 mbd in 1979, representing an increase of nearly 30 per cent. Oil revenues had also risen by 97.2 per cent from $10.8 billion to $21.3 billion during the same period. In the first nine months of 1980, oil revenues had increased further to $22.4 billion.

In all, Iraq was going through a period of 'never had it so good', with years of sustained economic growth, the building of its infrastructure, and a rapid and unparalleled rise in oil exports and revenues. Iraq had also started to build up new infrastructure and facilities in preparation for hosting the Non-Aligned Conference in September 1982 in Baghdad and had, by the time of the invasion, accumulated at least $35 billion in foreign-exchange reserves.

Therefore, when analysing the impact of the war on Iraq, it must be noted that, in contrast to Iran, Iraq, at the time of the war, was at its apex of development and modernization, with a promising future ahead of it.

Table 3.1 Oil production and major recipient of Iraq's oil exports 1973-85 (thousand tonnes)

	1973	1974	1975*	1976	1977	1978	1979	1980
Oil production	99,400	102,900	110,100	117,300	122,100	125,500	170,300	130,000
Oil export	89,200	98,000	100,100	110,000	112,900	116,800	160,400	120,400
Destination:								
USA	205	–	95	1,544	4,010	3,039	4,514	1,636
Canada	1,057	471	1,639	1,427	917	1,200	415	956
West Germany	1,613	3,570	1,404	1,734	1,114	2,913	2,233	2,943
UK	2,762	3,815	3,064	5,880	5,616	8,664	6,963	4,310
Italy	18,491	13,429	18,688	15,630	14,235	18,952	24,549	11,783
France	18,678	16,739	12,018	16,812	18,234	20,537	24,449	23,262
Netherlands	652	456	1,940	3,015	3,342	3,677	1,976	656
Belgium	818	362	1,617	1,254	2,202	1,876	2,427	1,660
Spain	2,327	3,408	6,032	3,857	5,586	5,962	5,831	6,171
Japan	111	1,871	4,650	6,654	7,355	7,973	12,703	15,863
Australia	1,663	–	1,227	570	1,806	1,500	1,009	183
Turkey	3,107	4,219	7,610	6,614	6,600	8,664	6,963	3,957
Others (including Eastern bloc countries)*	37,716	49,660	40,116	45,009	41,883	31,943	66,368	47,020

Table 3.1 (continued)

	1981	1982	1983	1984	1985	% share of total exports*			
						1973	1978	1979	1985
Oil production	43,900	49,600	53,800	59,800	68,778				
Oil export	34,100	39,300	32,500	35,500	48,549				
Destination:									
USA	539	132	510	627	2,322	0.2	2.6	3.0	5.0
Canada	0	0	0	0	0	1.2	1.0	0.2	0.0
West Germany	2,423	779	1,472	1,989	329	1.8	2.5	1.0	0.7
UK	5,549	5,447	622	413	1,964	3.1	7.4	4.0	4.0
Italy	7,674	5,715	4,865	4,532	6,243	20.7	16.2	15.0	13.0
France	2,282	1,474	1,998	3,257	6,428	20.9	17.6	15.0	13.0
Netherlands	0	2,877	141	1,038	1,290	0.7	3.1	1.0	3.0
Belgium	51	407	1,611	1,856	732	0.9	1.6	2.0	2.0
Spain	2,277	2,875	2,071	3,176	5,692	2.6	5.0	4.0	12.0
Japan	2,914	3,285	470	471	3,103	0.1	6.8	8.0	6.0
Australia	465	0	0	0	0	1.8	1.3	0.6	0.0
Turkey	392	1,016	4,374	4,072	5,631	3.5	7.4	4.0	12.0
Others (including Eastern bloc countries)*	9,534	15,293	14,366	14,069	14,815	42.3	27.3	41.0	31.0

Note: * Author's calculations. All the percentages have been rounded up and therefore totals may not add to 100.
Sources: Statistiques 1974–86;
United Nations International Economic and Social Affairs (1979–83) Yearbook of World Energy Statistics
OECD 1974–86

The impact of the war on oil production and exports

By far the most severe blow to the economy of Iraq as a result of the war has been to the oil sector. Within the first few days of the war the Iraqi refinery at Basra, off-loading facilities at Fao, Khor al-Amaya and Mina al-Bakr, as well as the key K-1 pumping stations in the Kirkuk field in the north, were put out of action. Thus, within a week of the outbreak of the hostilities, Iraq was forced to suspend virtually all its oil exports.

The significant decline in oil production/exports can best be seen in table 3.1 and figure 3.1, where the volume of oil production and its exports during the 1973–85 period are noted. As can be seen, oil production decreased by 24 and 66 per cent between 1979/80 and 1980/1, where it fell from 170,300 thousand tonnes in 1979 to 130,000 thousand tonnes in 1980 and then fell drastically to only 43,900 thousand tonnes in 1981. Since 1982 the situation has improved somewhat, although not rising to anything nearing the pre-war levels. By 1985 and 1986 oil production had increased to 68,778 and 82,665 thousand tonnes (Statistiques 1986).

In all, on average each year, oil production has declined by 9.7 per cent between 1979 and 1986. The corresponding figure for the pre-war period of 1973–9 was an increase of 9.4 per cent.

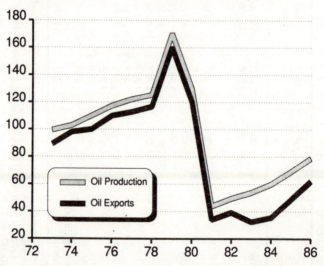

Figure 3.1 Oil production and exports: Iraq, 1973–86 (million tonnes)
Sources: *Statistiques* 1974–86; United Nations International Economic and Social Affairs (1979–83) *Yearbook of World Energy Statistics*; OECD 1974–86

The decline in oil production has resulted in a massive reduction in oil exports. The export of oil fell by 25 per cent between 1979 and 1980. The corresponding figure for the 1980/1 period was 72 per cent, where oil exports fell from 120,400 thousand in 1980 to only 34,100 thousand tonnes in 1981. Then, as a result of improvements in oil production, oil exports were also increased, and by 1985 48,549 thousand tonnes of oil were exported. The corresponding figure for 1986 is 62,100 thousand tonnes (Statistiques 1986).

In all, during 1979 to 1986, oil exports have declined by 12.7 per cent on average each year, while, during 1973–9, the corresponding figure was an increase of 10.3 per cent.

Therefore, it can be seen that one of the most serious consequences of the war has been in the oil sector, where oil production/exports have declined significantly, while every effort has been made to increase them.

With regard to the main recipients of oil exports, it can be said that all the countries mentioned in table 3.1 have reduced their overall imports of Iraqi oil (i.e. they have reduced their dependency on Iraq).

The importance of oil in providing foreign exchange during the period under study and the failure of the Iraqi government to achieve one of the main objectives of its planning policies, namely, reducing the country's dependency on oil revenues as the main supplier of foreign exchange, and also to increase non-energy exports, as outlined for example in the Five-Year National Development Plan, 1981/85 (Plan and Budget Organization 1982), can best be seen in table 3.2, where the value of total exports and its composition during the 1973–86 period are given.

As can be noted, given the serious damages to oil-export facilities, the revenue generated by petroleum exports has fallen drastically. It fell from 7,718 million dinars in 1980 to only 2,752 million dinars in 1986, representing an average annual decline of 16 per cent during the same period. The value of non-energy exports has remained more or less static at around 40–42 million dinars a year. It should, however, be noted that in both cases the figures quoted are in current prices. Therefore, if inflation is taken into consideration, the actual decline in constant prices during the period under study can be very substantial indeed.

At this point, if the pre- and post-war foreign-exchange earnings are compared, it can be seen that, during the 1973–9 period, Iraqi oil revenues as well as its total export earnings continuously increased each year. The average annual rates of increase were 50 and 48 per cent respectively.

Table 3.2 Value of Iraq's total exports, 1973–86 (million current dinars)

	1973	1974	1975	1976	1977	1978	1979	1980	1981	1982	1983	1984	1985	1986
TX	588	1,949	2,450	2,738	2,850	3,266	6,329	7,760	3,110	3,056	3,042	3,545	3,903	2,792
CPX	555	1,921	2,415	2,692	2,807	3,204	6,287	7,718	3,068	3,014	3,000	3,495	3,862	2,752
N-EX*	33	28	35	46	43	62	42	42	42	42	42	50	44	40
Share of CPX in TX*	% 94.4	% 98.6	% 98.6	% 98.3	% 98.5	% 98.1	% 99.3	% 99.4	% 98.6	% 98.6	% 98.6	% 98.6	% 99.0	% 99.0
Share of N-EX in TX*	% 5.6	% 1.4	% 1.4	% 1.7	% 1.5	% 1.9	% 0.7	% 0.6	% 1.4	% 1.4	% 1.4	% 1.4	% 1.0	% 1.0

Notes: * Author's calculation.
TX Total exports.
CPX Crude petroleum exports.
N-EX Non-energy exports.
The exchange rate for the period under study: $1 = 0.30 dinars (1973), 0.29 (1974–82) and 0.31 (1983–6).

Sources: IMFa 1987
Statistiques 1986

The impact of the war on the value, composition and the origins of non-defence imports

The money value of Iraq's total imports during the 1973–85 period, like those of Iran, has been the subject of much fluctuation. However, at the outset it should be noted that, at least for the first two years of the war, Saddam Hussain, with the help of his friends in the region, was a man determined to have both guns and butter. As it will be shown in a later chapter, not only has the value of military expenditures (Milex) increased significantly since the war, but there was also a rapid increase in non-military imports in the early years of the invasion.

Given the drastic fall in Iraq's foreign exchange earnings, the simultaneous increases in Milex, arms imports and non-defence imports would not have been possible without outside help. Two Arab countries, amongst others, have become indispensable to Iraq's war efforts. They are Saudi Arabia and Kuwait. Both have played a primary role in sustaining Iraq's economy.

It has been estimated that Arab-source financial support for Iraq, mainly from Saudi Arabia and Kuwait, during the first two years of the war amounted to $1.0 billion a month (for evidence on this statement see, for example, Karsh 1987, Goose 1987, Stauffer 1985). This undoubtedly enabled Iraq to follow a policy of not only 'guns and butter', but also with added honey and jam.

Indeed the government in Baghdad deliberately set out to accelerate the pace of economic development and went to considerable effort in the first two years of the invasion to cushion the population and to ensure that the average Iraqi citizen would not suffer economically because of the war.

Furthermore, the scale of government expenditures and imports during this period becomes even more clear when we note that, in spite of all the outside financial help, by the end of 1982/3 Iraq had still exhausted its $35.0 billion foreign-exchange reserves and had become a major debtor nation, a point to which we shall return in a future chapter.

Table 3.3 provides data on the money value of total non-military imports between 1973 and 1985. As can be seen, the value of imports was $8,984 million in 1979, increasing to $14,067 million in 1980, $20,922 million in 1981 and still increasing to an all-time high of $21,728 million in 1982, representing an average annual growth rate of 32.2 per cent during the same period.

However, two years into the war, Saddam Hussain had not delivered the goods, as Khomeini was still in charge in Iran, while the burden of supporting the Iraqis was ever increasing. Thus the

Table 3.3 Value and distribution of Iraq's imports[a] by main countries, 1973–85 (million current dollars)

	1973	1974	1975	1976	1977	1978	1979	1980
USA	50	188	370	218	218	426	486	797
Canada	2	22	79	72	71	10	99	137
West Germany	36	191	754	848	802	476	1,258	1,980
UK	78	126	238	273	307	261	470	823
Italy	30	79	164	192	228	217	741	1,037
France	76	175	263	309	252	296	877	1,179
Netherlands	14	38	61	75	184	80	260	275
Belgium	39	53	99	70	106	110	315	374
Switzerland	12	29	48	40	85	141	152	233
Sweden	17	54	92	82	62	119	353	397
Spain	20	22	45	33	45	56	159	213
Japan	61	270	765	518	789	881	1,759	2,413
Australia	4	89	45	98	88	51	204	221
Turkey	19	32	24	31	58	52	116	148
India	18	56	71	57	61	38	75	75
Brazil	53	131	200	77	70	48	264	318
Others (including Soviet Union and Eastern Europe)[b]	365	816	897	904	1,055	951	1,316	3,447
Total non-military imports	894	2,371	4,215	3,897	4,481	4,213	8,984	14,067

Table 3.3 *(continued)*

	1981	1982	1983	1984	1985	% share of total imports[b]			
						1973	1978	1979	1985
USA	1,005	931	563	731	470	6	10	5	4
Canada	198	173	105	140	57	0	0	1	0.5
West Germany	3,179	3,452	1,618	947	926	4	11	14	9
UK	1,382	1,698	669	500	630	9	6	5	6
Italy	1,475	1,827	878	691	760	3	5	8	7
France	1,601	1,588	894	752	757	9	7	10	7
Netherlands	314	322	175	187	181	2	2	3	2
Belgium	351	371	175	146	132	4	3	4	1
Switzerland	298	369	220	112	118	1	3	2	1
Sweden	626	519	144	116	137	2	3	4	1
Spain	306	299	102	133	107	2	1	2	1
Japan	3,324	3,019	695	884	1,450	7	21	20	14
Australia	106	221	99	216	177	0	1	2	2
Turkey	615	672	352	1,028	822	2	1	1	8
India	86	95	85	77	61	2	1	0.8	0.6
Brazil	328	350	453	385	699	6	1	3	7
Others (including Soviet Union and Eastern Europe)[b]	5,728	5,882	5,048	4,133	3,050	41	23	15	29
Total non-military imports	20,922	21,728	12,275	11,178	10,534	100	100	100	100

Notes: [a] Excluding military-related imports.
[b] Author's calculation, all the percentages have been rounded up, thus totals may not add up to 100.
Sources: IMFb 1980, 1983, 1986
IMFa 1986

Arab financiers of Iraq's war efforts changed their tactics by reducing their direct 'loan' of cash to Iraq (except for the payments of arms deliveries by the Soviet Union which is directly paid for by the Saudis) in favour of exporting 300,000 barrels of oil a day from the Neutral Zone on behalf of Iraq (Stauffer 1985). (This issue is noted further in chapter ten.)

The reduction in total cash support, as well as the exhaustion of the foreign-exchange reserves, reduced Iraq's ability to sustain high levels of imports. Indeed, between 1982–3, 1983–4 and 1984–5 the value of imports fell by 44, 9 and 6 per cent respectively. By 1986, total imports had fallen further to only $8,847 million (IMF 1987b).

Such a decline in imports and the fact that Iraq's industrialization, like that of Iran, has been based on 'dependent capitalism' and the import-substitution strategy of development, with its massive import requirements, must have created many problems and set-backs in the economy.

At this point, it should be noted that the government of Iraq has not published much data and information on different aspects of the economy since the war. However, it can be argued that the consequences of the war itself, i.e. dislocation of the labour force, flight of the educated people, reduction in foreign workers, etc., as well as the significant reduction in imports, have meant that the industry is operating far below its actual potential. Also now, more than ever before, consumer-goods imports form a very large share of the total imports with no apparent contribution to the development of the domestic economy.

Table 3.4 provides figures for the share of non-military imports in GDP. As can be seen, in 1979, the share of imports in GDP (including oil) was 22.8 per cent. However, given the reduction in GDP since the war, as well as the massive increase in imports, by 1982 the corresponding share had increased to 50 per cent. In all, during 1979 to 1985 on average each year the burden of imports has amounted to 32.5 per cent of the GDP (including oil).

If the above figures are compared with the pre-war ones, it can clearly be noted that indeed, since the war, there has been an unprecedented increase in Iraq's import dependency. For example, during the 1973–8 period, on average each year, Iraq had spent 2.9 per cent of its GDP (including oil) on its non-defence imports.

Therefore it can be argued that one of the major consequences of the war for Iraq has been the rapid and significant increase in its import dependency. As noted in chapter one, the Iraqi strategy of development and modernization during the post-oil-price-increase period of 1973–4 was mainly based on a 'less big' approach to development.

Table 3.4 Iraq's share of non-military imports in GDP* (oil inclusive and oil exclusive) 1973–85

	1973	1974	1975	1976	1977	1978	1979	1980	1981	1982	1983	1984	1985
Total non-military imports	0.058	0.083	0.123	0.138	0.172	0.205	2.6	4.1	6.1	6.3	3.8	3.5	3.3
GDP (including oil) (a)	1.6	3.4	4.0	5.2	5.9	7.0	11.4	15.8	11.1	12.6	13.1	13.9	16.8
Import/GDP ratio % *	3.6	2.4	3.1	2.6	2.9	2.9	22.8	25.9	54.9	50.0	29.0	25.2	20.0
GDP (excluding oil) (b)	0.65	1.3	1.6	2.1	2.3	2.8	5.0	6.0	7.9	5.1	6.6	7.6	10.8
Import/GDP ratio % *	8.9	6.4	7.7	6.6	7.5	7.3	52.1	68.3	77.2	123.5	57.6	46.0	30.6

	%
Average share/year (a) 1973–8*	2.9
Average share/year (b) 1973–8*	7.4
Average share/year (a) 1979–85*	32.5
Average share/year (b) 1979–85*	65.0

Notes: * Author's calculation. The figures for total non-military imports and GDP are in current billion dinars.
Sources: IMFb 1980, 1986; IMFa 1980, 1986; United Nations Economic and Social Commission for Western Asia 1981 and Republic of Iraq 1983; United Nations Economic and Social Commission for Western Asia 1986

Thus it can be said that, given the past policies, it is most likely that, during the post-1979-oil-price-increase period, if the war had not taken place, Iraq would not have increased its non-defence imports so significantly. Therefore, not only would she not have exhausted her foreign-exchange reserves, but, also by now, the actual $35.0 billion of reserves would have increased a few times over.

In our analysis so far we have used the current values of imports. We now analyse constant-price figures. The data on the value of total imports at 1974 constant prices has been calculated by using the index of industrial countries' export values, whose figures are given in table 3.5. As can be seen, the value of non-military imports at 1974 constant prices was 1.6 billion dinars in 1979, rising significantly to 3.8 billion dinars in 1982.

Since 1982, however, given the decline in imports at current prices, there has also been a decline in constant-price figures. They fell to 2.4 billion dinars in 1983 and still further to only 1.6 billion dinars in 1986.

In all, between 1979 and 1986, there has been a zero growth in imports at 1974 constant prices. The corresponding figure for the 1979–82 period, to take account of the drastic fall in imports between 1982 and 1986, is the rise of 33.4 per cent on average each year, while the figure for the 1982–6 period is a decline of 19.5 per cent on average each year. Total imports at 1974 constant prices during the pre-war period of 1973–8 had increased by 15.5 per cent on average each year.

At this point, the origins of Iraq's imports (non-military) since the war, whose data was provided in table 3.3, is the subject of analysis. As can be seen, it seems that between 1979 and 1982, all the countries mentioned in the table had decided to reward Iraq for invading Iran by exporting as much as they could to that country. For example, Iraq's imports from the USA, West Germany, the UK, Italy, France and Japan increased by 24, 40, 53, 35, 22 and 20 per cent respectively on average each year during the same period.

Furthermore, by looking at the figures given in table 3.3, it can be noted that, during the post-war period of 1980–5, Japan has remained the major supplier of Iraq's non-military imports, supplying 14 per cent of the total in 1985, followed by Germany (9 per cent), Turkey (8 per cent), Italy and France (7 per cent) each and the UK (6 per cent).

If the above figures are compared with those of 1979 (i.e. before the invasion), the biggest major change that can be noted is in the value of imports from Turkey, as in that year

Table 3.5 Estimation of Iraq's non-military imports at 1974 constant prices,* 1973–86 (billion constant dinars)

	1973	1974	1975	1976	1977	1978	1979	1980	1981	1982	1983	1984	1985	1986
Total non-military imports (current prices)	0.058	0.083	0.123	0.138	0.172	0.205	2.6	4.1	6.1	6.2	3.8	3.5	3.3	2.7
Index of industrial countries' export values 1974 = 1	0.8	1.0	1.1	1.1	1.2	1.4	1.6	1.8	1.7	1.7	1.6	1.5	1.5	1.7
Total non-military imports at 1974 constant prices	0.073	0.083	0.111	0.123	0.142	0.150	1.6	2.3	3.5	3.8	2.4	2.3	2.2	1.6

	1973–8	1979–86	1979–82	1982–6
Average annual growth of non-military imports at constant 1974 prices (%)*	15.5	0	33.4	−19.5

Note: * Author's calculation.
Sources: IMFb Direction of Trade Statistics, 1980, 1987; IMFa International Financial Statistics, 1980, 1986

Turkey had accounted for only 0.8 per cent of Iraq's total imports.

The rapid increase in trade with Turkey is an important issue which should be analysed further. As noted in chapter two, Turkey has also become a major trading partner of Iran, ever since the war, importing vast quantities of oil and exporting a large volume of merchandise in exchange.

This has meant that, while Turkey has been receiving oil from both Iran and Iraq, she has been selling to them goods and services which might not have been sold elsewhere, i.e. in the Western world, with such ease.

Therefore trade of this kind must have been greatly advantageous to Turkey, leading to much improvement in her foreign-exchange earnings and economic well-being. However, when the war ends, the result could be a serious economic blow to Turkey, should Iran and Iraq decide to curtail their trade with that country.

Thus, if events follow this scenario, the peace might bring economic hardship or even instability to those countries that have greatly benefited from the war and have become dependent on trade with Iran and Iraq.

The impact of the war on the agricultural sector

The potential of the agricultural sector in Iraq is substantial, both in terms of abundant agricultural land and also availability of ample water resources, mainly from the Tigris and Euphrates rivers. In 1980 the importance and potential of agriculture in Iraq's overall development was once more highlighted when Saddam Hussain declared that agriculture was Iraq's 'permanent oil' and that he wanted to see the country become self-sufficient and a net exporter of food within this century (see further Turkuje Sinai Kalkinma Barkasi 1983). However, this statement was made before he ordered his army to invade Iran.

At this point therefore it is appropriate to note what has been happening to the agricultural sector since the war, especially in terms of production and imports/exports of agricultural commodities.

The figures for the estimated production of principal crop products and main livestock items between 1973 and 1985 are given in table 3.6. As can be noted, the average annual rate of production of many items such as wheat, rice, corn and bovine meat has fallen significantly during the 1979–85 period. The production of dates which has traditionally provided the major share of non-energy exports has drastically fallen from 581 thousand

Table 3.6 Estimated production of principal agricultural products and main livestock items, Iraq, 1973–85 (thousand metric tonnes)*

	1973	1974	1975	1976	1977	1978	1979	1980	1981	1982	1983	1984	1985
Wheat	957	1,339	845	1,312	696	910	1,492	1,300	1,100	965	841	471	650
Rice	157	68	200	163	199	172	284	250	250	163	111	109	105
Barley	462	533	437	579	458	602	620	575	600	550	700	482	700
Corn	19	20	20	55	82	85	100	90	90	28	28	31	32
Dates	385	350	400	372	578	581	392	395	405	374	345	251	100
Sugar cane	98	100	100	128	152	160	210	260	260	146	82	86	85
Bovine meat	50	45	41	47	48	49	51	52	53	36	34	40	35
Mutton and lamb	32	34	34	39	37	38	37	38	38	48	48	55	50
Poultry	26	27	29	34	35	36	37	38	41	155	113	125	150
Cows' milk	254	253	254	255	245	252	255	259	265	301	319	336	300
Sheep milk	124	125	125	130	125	126	129	130	130	165	165	165	168
Butter	10	11	11	11	10	10	7	7	7	8	8	7	8
Cheese	34	50	50	50	26	26	27	27	27	33	33	32	33

Note: * Figure rounded to the nearest 1,000 tonnes.
Sources: FAOa 1975, 1979, 1981, 1984, 1985

tonnes in 1978 to only 100 thousand tonnes in 1985, representing an average rate of decline of 23 per cent each year.

At this point, if the pre- and post-war figures of agricultural production are compared, it can be argued that, although the pre-war performance was far from being perfect, none the less, by looking at the figures, there can be no doubt that since the war there has been a major deterioration in agricultural productivity.

Given the scope of this study, it is not possible to provide a detailed study of the reasons for the poor performance of the agricultural sector. However, as with Iran, there can be no doubt that the mounting costs of the war and the increased rural–urban migration caused by it[1] are amongst the main reasons for the increased deterioration of the agricultural sector.

Table 3.7 provides figures for imports of principal agricultural products and main livestock items from 1973 to 1985. As can be seen, since the war, the imports of all the items mentioned in the table, except for barley, has significantly increased during the period under study. It is also important to note that since the war Iraq has become much more dependent on the outside world for its basic food supplies (see further table 3.7).

In all, as with Iran, the failure of the agricultural sector to provide food for a growing population and to reduce the country's overall dependency on the outside world for food, can, in our view, be identified as another major consequence of the war.

Conclusion

In this chapter we have looked mainly at some of the major economic consequences of the war on Iraq during the 1980–5 period. It was noted that, on the eve of the invasion, Iraq was enjoying a period of 'never had it so good', with years of sustained economic growth, a rapid and unparalleled increase in oil production/exports and revenues.

However, through our analysis, it has been established that there has been very serious deterioration in all aspects of the economy since the war, with oil production/exports and revenues suffering most.

We also noted that, since the war, there has been a massive increase in Iraq's import dependency, rising from 2.9 per cent of GDP (including oil) between 1973 and 1978 to 32.5 per cent in the 1979–85 period. It was also demonstrated that, since the war, there has been a major deterioration of the agricultural sector, leading to decreases in agricultural production and consequently an increase in food imports.

Table 3.7 Imports of principal agricultural products and main livestock items, Iraq, 1973–8 (thousand metric tonnes)+

	1973	1974	1975	1976	1977	1978	1979	1980	1981	1982	1983	1984	1985
Wheat and flour	154	672	512	616	723	997	1,806	1,698	1,615	2,247	2,627	3,317	2,317
Rice	16	198	120	194	235	180	320	345	350	370	440	487	500
Barley	–	–	25	24	127	163	274	233	110	165	270	500	160
Corn	–	–	–	6	26	86	150	125	200	70	190	346	408
Sugar (total raw equivalent)	474	427	378	329	480	428	513	737	517	542	488	523	611
Sugar (refined)	188	121	159	181	197	180	107	229	200	287	304	367	562
Bovine meat (fresh/frozen)	0.2	10	1	–	–	9	7	10	21	80	70	80	85
Sheep meat (fresh/frozen)	–	6	–	–	15	3	14	14	31	20	16	35	30
Poultry (dry, fresh cond.)	0.2	0.8	1	5	18	18	55	100	173	140	85	70	75
Milk	1	11	8	17	18	19	41	39	54	39	44	53	63
Butter	0.4	2	1	3	5	5	5	6	9	4	6	7	8
Cheese	1	4	4	3	3	4	15	20	20	30	15	32	33

Note: + Figure rounded to nearest 1,000 tonnes.
Sources: FAOb 1975, 1978, 1979, 1981, 1984, 1985

In all, the failure to achieve any of the main objectives of planning in general, and the deterioration of the economy as a whole, can be said to be some of the major consequences of the war.

The chapter also noted that, since the war, Turkey has become a major trading partner of both Iran and Iraq, importing vast quantities of oil and exporting a large volume of merchandise in exchange.

It was then argued that, while Turkey has been receiving oil from Iran and Iraq, she has been selling to them goods and services which might not have been sold elsewhere, i.e. in the Western world, with such ease.

Furthermore it was also contended that trade of this kind must have been greatly advantageous to Turkey, leading to improvements in her foreign-exchange capabilities and economic well-being. However, should Iran and Iraq decide to curtail their trade with Turkey, when the war ends, and spend their moneys on importing high technology and higher-quality goods and services from the West instead, then the result could be a serious economic blow to that country, causing much economic hardship or even instability.

Chapter four

Militarization of Iran 1973–8: an economic analysis

Introduction

One of the most significant consequences of the oil-price increases on 1973–4 was a rapid growth in military expenditure in the Middle Eastern oil-exporting countries. The biggest military build-up was in Iran which by the mid-1970s had become the 'absolute' military power in the Gulf.

Military expenditure (Milex), arms imports and attempts to militarize a country are controversial areas of study. There are different 'pull' and 'push' factors causing them. Factors such as 'security', 'stability', 'image', 'linkage' with 'development', 'modernity' and 'regional design' can be named as just a few (for further reading see Arlinghaus 1984, especially chapter three).

A peculiarity of high Milex in the Middle East, which has a serious effect on the political economy of these countries, is its very high import content. There are two main reasons for this. One is that, after the oil-price increases, the 'petro-dollars' had to be recycled. Therefore arming the oil-exporting countries became a means by which the said objective could be achieved.

Thus, in contrast to a not too distant past, i.e. before the early 1970s when most of the military imports were part of the total military-aid package of the suppliers, the arms importers became responsible for the payment for their military imports. This obviously has changed the character of recent military transfers and has put the burden of military imports on to the recipient countries (see further Palme 1982: 4–21).

Second, given the sums involved, and the scale of arms transfers envisaged, arms sales became in many ways the principal instrument of foreign policy in the Third World (Arlinghaus 1984* 4–21). As Andrew Pierre (1981/2: 4–21) has noted, 'Arms sales have become more now than ever before, a crucial dimension of world politics. They are now major strands in the warp and woof of international affairs. Arms sales are far more than an economic occurrence, a military relationship or an arms control challenge – *arms sales are foreign policy writ large'* (emphasis in original).

The above is a brief presentation of some of the important reasons concerning 'pull' and 'push' factors causing high Milex and arms imports. Given the scope of this chapter and the limits of our coverage, we shall not attempt to provide a detailed and comprehensive study of topics such as politico-strategic, military 'domestic' or 'foreign' objectives of a rapid increase in militarization.[1] What we intend to do is to provide a brief study of the economic consequences of such expenditures on Iran and Iraq.

Therefore, in this and in the following chapters, we will note the defence burden, estimate the value of arms imports and provide data on the measurement of arms-imports burdens. The major arms agreements and the main arms suppliers will be identified. The rate at which different countries in the Gulf have been militarized, measured by the changes in the numbers of military personnel, as well as the availability of main military hardware, will be noted. Analysis of these topics will start in this chapter, where Iran's experience with rapid militarization during the 1973–8 period is given.

The estimation of defence and arms-imports burdens

The figures for Milex and defence burden – that is, the share of military expenditure (Milex) in GDP during 1973–8 are given in table 4.1. As can be noted, during the period under study, Milex

Table 4.1 Ratio of military expenditures (Milex) in GDP* (oil including and excluding) – defence burden, Iran, 1973–8

	Milex	GDP (including oil)	Share of defence in GDP (%)	GDP (excluding oil)	Share of defence in GDP (%)
1973	145	1,784	8.1	1,196	12.1
1974	218	3,072	7.1	1,630	13.3
1975	707	3,479	20.3	2,130	33.6
1976	665	4,480	14.8	2,820	23.7
1977	561	5,207	10.7	3,545	15.8
1978	693	4,917	14.1	3,692	18.7

Average annual growth of Milex (%) (1973–8)	Average defence burden (%) 1973–8	
37.0	in GDP (including oil)	in GDP (excluding oil)
	13.0	19.9

Notes: * Author's calculation. The figures for Milex and GDP are in current billion rials.
Source: Based on Mofid 1987: 181, table 5.2

increased from 145 billion rials in 1973 to 693 billion rials in 1978 which represents a 37 per cent average annual increase for the period.

The highest rate of increase in Milex was between 1974 and 1975, where it increased by more than 224 per cent. This, in our view, clearly demonstrates the relationship between the militarization of Iran, and the petro-dollar-recycling objective of the arms sale. Furthermore, the share defence in GDP (including oil) increased from 8.1 per cent in 1973 to 14.1 per cent in 1978.

At this point, if we compare the above sets of figures with those of selected countries whose figures are given in table 4.2, we can indeed note the scale at which Iran had become militarized during the period under observation.

Table 4.2 World military expenditures (Milex) as percentage of GDP*, selected countries, 1973–8

	1973	1974	1975	1976	1977	1978
Canada	1.9	1.9	1.9	1.8	1.9	2.0
USA	6.0	6.1	6.0	5.4	5.4	5.2
Belgium	2.8	2.8	3.1	3.1	3.2	3.3
Denmark	2.1	2.3	2.5	2.3	2.3	2.4
France	3.8	3.7	3.8	3.8	3.9	3.9
FR Germany	3.5	3.6	3.6	3.5	3.4	3.4
Greece	4.1	4.3	6.5	5.9	6.8	6.6
Italy	2.9	2.8	2.5	2.3	2.4	2.4
Turkey	4.3	4.1	6.0	6.4	6.0	5.5
UK	4.8	5.0	4.9	5.0	4.8	4.7
India	3.0	3.0	3.3	3.4	3.2	3.1
Pakistan	6.1	6.0	6.1	5.6	5.4	5.3
Indonesia	3.7	3.1	4.1	3.9	4.1	4.3
Japan	0.8	0.9	0.9	0.9	0.9	0.9
Australia	2.4	2.5	2.5	2.5	2.5	2.5

Note: * GDP at current market prices.
Source: SIPRI 1981: 166–7 Table 6A.4

As can be seen, countries such as Canada, USA, UK, Indonesia (i.e. oil-exporting economies outside the Middle East), Greece and Turkey, India and Pakistan (both sets of countries with a long history of conflict) were spending between 3 and 7 per cent of their GDP on Milex. (For further details see table 4.2.)

As was mentioned earlier, one of the peculiarities of Milex in the oil-rich economies of the Middle East has been its very high import content. During the period under study Iran became the main importer of major weapons in the region. This can clearly be seen in table 4.3, where rank order of major Middle East arms importers during 1970–4 and 1975–9 is given.

Table 4.3 Rank order of major Middle East arms importers, 1970–4 and 1975–9

	Middle East % of Third World total	Largest recipient countries	% of region's total	Largest supplier to each country	% of country's total	The four largest suppliers of the region	% of the region's total
1970–4	50	Syria	25	Soviet Union	95	Soviet Union	51
		Egypt	23	Soviet Union	98	USA	34
		Iran	22	USA	60	UK	10
		Israel	18	USA	97	France	2
		Iraq	4	Soviet Union	85		
		Saudi Arabia	3	USA	51		
1975–9	48	Iran	31	USA	81	USA	61
		Saudi Arabia	14	USA	79	Soviet Union	15
		Jordan	13	USA	98	France	7
		Iraq	12	Soviet Union	85	UK	5
		Israel	10	USA	95		
		Syria	6	Soviet Union	84		

Sources: Based on SIPRI 1980: 96–7, tables 3.6 and 3.7

While in 1970–4 Iran was the third largest importer of weapons in the Middle East (after Syria and Egypt), by the 1975–9 period it had become the largest, importing 31 per cent of the region's total weapon imports, only a few percentage points less than the combined imports of Saudi Arabia, Iraq and Syria. It is also important to note that, during the 1973–4 and 1975–8 periods, the USA had supplied 60 and 81 per cent of Iran's total arms imports. We shall return to this point once more, when the value of Iran's arms imports is the subject of study.

Table 4.4 provides data on the estimated values of Iran's arms imports, as well as the ratio of arms imports to total imports; that is, the trade burden of arms imports during 1973–8. As can be noted, the value of arms imports increased from 87 billion rials in 1973 to 416 billion rials in 1978, representing a 37 per cent average annual increase during the same period.

An important point to note is the fact that arms imports had increased from 87 billion rials in 1973 to 424 billion rials in 1975, representing a 121 per cent average annual increase. This observation is another example of the direct relationship between the oil-price increases of 1973–4 and arms sales as a way of recycling petro-dollars back into the advanced economies.

As for the arms-import burdens, as can be seen, the ratio had increased from 26 per cent in 1973 to 37 per cent in 1978. In all, the trade burden of arms imports was 29.5 per cent on average each

Table 4.4 Ratio of arms imports in total imports (burden of arms imports)[a], Iran, 1973–8

	Arms Imports[b] A	Non-Defence Import B	Total Imports (A) + (B)	Ratio of arms imports/ total imports (%) $\dfrac{A}{(A) + (B)} \times 100$
1973	87	248	335	26.0
1974	131	442	573	22.9
1975	424	782	1,206	35.2
1976	399	875	1,274	31.3
1977	337	1,022	1,359	24.8
1978	416	721	1,137	37.0

Average annual growth of arms imports 1973–8: 37.0 per cent

Average annual growth of arms imports burden 1973–8: 29.5 per cent

Notes: [a] Author's calculation.
   [b] For the way in which arms imports have been estimated see Mofid 1987.
   The figures quoted for defence and non-defence imports are in current billion rials.
Sources: Based on Mofid 1987: table 3.1; 183: table 5.3

year during the same period; a substantial increase by historical standards. For example, between 1968 and 1972 the arms-import burden ratio had increased by 12.2 per cent on average each year (for evidence see Mofid 1987: 183, table 5.3).

Given the sums involved, it would be very interesting to note what Iran had received in exchange for such an impressive payment. The shopping list (i.e. the arms agreements) negotiated between Iran and the US, the UK, France, the Soviet Union, Italy and the Netherlands are shown in tables 4.7–9 at the end of the chapter. Because of the revolution, the hostage crisis, and the war with Iraq, not all the items noted in these tables have been delivered. None the less, they establish beyond any doubt the extent to which Iran's militarization process was in progress. Later on, we shall provide the list of major weapon items that had been supplied by the time of the Shah's downfall.

These tables present some interesting observations. The US was the only supplier of fighter planes. They also supplied the majority of helicopters and air transport tankers. Destroyers and submarines were also US supplied, as were some of the tanks. The UK provided Chieftain and Scorpion tanks and many armoured carriers and ships.

France and the Netherlands provided transport aircraft and frigates. Missiles of all sorts were mostly supplied by the US, followed by the UK and France. Strangely enough, even the Soviet Union (the main supplier of Iraq) had joined the Western nations in selling arms to the Shah). They provided surface-to-air missiles (SAM), guns and armoured carriers.

As was mentioned earlier, not all the items ordered by the Shah had been delivered by the time of the revolution. However, the following is an attempt to identify the weapons that were in service in Iran by 1979.

Table 4.5 illustrates major weapon systems held by the Iranian armed forces in 1972/3 and 1979/80. As can be seen, the numbers of tanks, combat aircraft and helicopters had increased from 960, 160 and 140 to 1985, 445 and 684 respectively during the same period.

In all, by 1979/80, the army, in addition to the previously held American-supplied tanks, had received 875 Chieftain and 250 Scorpion tanks from Britain, armed with many different types of missiles. The armour was strengthened by the addition of 100 radar-controlled anti-aircraft guns, Hawk surface-to-air missiles, as well as 570 helicopters of various types.

The navy had received 1 'Tang' submarine, 3 destroyers, 4 'Saam' frigates, 4 PF 103 Corvettes, 7 large patrol ships, 2 inshore

Table 4.5 Major weapons systems held by the armed forces, Iran, 1972/3–1979/80

	1972/3	*1979/80*
Tanks	960	1,985[a]
Combat aircraft	160	445[b]
Helicopters	140	684[c]
Armoured fighting vehicle	1,100	825

Notes: [a] Among them 875 were Chieftain, 250 Scorpion (both British supplied); the rest included 400 M-47/-48, and 460 M-60AI (American supplied).
[b] All American supplied; among them 190 F-4D/E, and 166 F-5E/F.
[c] Mostly American supplied.
Sources: IISS 1972/3 and 1979/80

minesweepers, 2 landing ships, 1 replenishment and 2 supply ships. The naval air force had 6 reconnaissance planes, 6 Sikorsky heavy helicopters, 20 SH–30 anti-submarine helicopters, and 24 helicopters of various types.

The air force had obtained 445 combat aircraft, among them 190 Phantoms, 166 Tiger 11, 77 Tomcat and 14 Phantom reconnaissance. It also had 13 Boeing 707 and 9 Boeing 747 tankers, as well as 84 helicopters of various types. The transport squadron included 18 E27s, 3 Aero Commander 690 and 4 Falcon 20. The fighters were armed with several different types of missiles, among them Phoenix, Sidewinder, Sparrow air-to-air missiles (AAM), Maverick and Condor air-to-ship missiles (ASM) (IISS 1978/9 and 1979/80).

In table 4.4, the estimated value of Iran's defence imports in billions of current rials was given. Given the yearly exchange rates,[2] the estimated values of arms imports in $US (current prices) were: $1.3 billion in 1973, $1.9 billion (1974), $6.2 billion (1975), $5.7 billion (1976), $4.7 billion (1977) and $5.9 billion (1978). Therefore the total estimated value of arms imports is $25.7 billion during the same period.

Moreover, as was noted earlier, in the 1973/4 and 1975/8 periods, the USA had supplied 60 and 81 per cent of Iran's total arms imports. Therefore, during the period under observation, the US had supplied $20 billion worth of arms to Iran. This is very important, as it shows the significance of the revolutionary leaders' action, when they cancelled most of the arms agreements with the US soon after the revolution, a point which we shall return to in chapter five.

At this point the scale of Iran's militarization, in terms of increases in military manpower during the 1972/3 to 1979/80 period (before the start of the Revolution) will be noted. As can be seen in table 4.6, the total military manpower increased from 191 thousand in 1972/3 to 415 thousand in 1979/80, representing an increase of 117 per cent during the same period.

Table 4.6 Military manpower and its composition, Iran, 1972/3–1979/80 (thousands)

	1972/3	*Change* [a] %	*1979/80*[b]
Total military manpower	191	117	415
of which:			
Army	160	78	285
Air Force	22	354	100
Navy	9	233	30
Paramilitary forces:			
gendarmerie	40	85	74

Notes: [a] Author's calculation.
[b] Relates to the period before the start of the revolution.
Sources: IISS 1972/3 and 1979/80

The highest percentage increase was in the air force where its manpower increased from 22,000 to 100,000 during the period under study. The air force was followed by the army and the navy respectively. There was also a major increase in the number of gendarmerie (paramilitary) forces.

Conclusion

In this chapter a brief study of the militarization of Iran during the period 1973–8 has been presented. It was noted that during the period under study 2,989 billion rials was spent on Milex. This sum represents a 13 per cent average annual share of GDP (including oil) during the period under observation. A large part of this expenditure was on 'ready-made' arms imports from abroad. Indeed, during this period, 1,794 billion rials was spent on importing, in off the shelf fashion, arms into Iran.

The chapter also clearly demonstrated the relationship between the massive increase in Iran's Milex/arms imports and the objective of the recycling of petro-dollars after the oil-price increases of 1973/4.

The militarization of Iran at break-neck speed was once described by Senator Frank Church as 'the most rapid build-up of military power under peace-time conditions of any nation in the history of the world' (Klare 1980: 12).

Such a build-up, especialy when it had linked the Shah so closely with US policies in the Gulf, had gone a long way to compromise the Shah's image with the Iranians. As Bani-Sadr noted at the time of the revolution:

> The economic health, social welfare and cultural integrity of the nation are all being sacrificed so that the Shah can continue to rule within the frame-work of American strategic objectives (Bani-Sadr 1978).

Given such an observation and feelings towards the Shah's militarization of Iran, it is no wonder that one of the first foreign-policy changes by the revolutionary leaders, was to bring an end to this policy and also to end the 'special' US–Iranian relations.

Table 4.7 US–Iranian arms agreements, 1973–9, by quantity, type and date of order[a]

Quantity[b]	Weapon designation	Weapon description	Year of order
80	Gruman F-14 Tomcat	Fighter/interceptor	1974
176	MCD–D F-4E Phantom	Fighter	1973, 1974
169	Northrop F-5E Tiger II	Fighter	1973, 1975
49	Beechcraft F33C Bonaza	Aircraft	1973, 1974
28	MCD-DRF-4E Phantom	Fighter/recce aircraft	1974, 1977, 1978
28	Northrop F-5F	Fighter/trainer	1975
160	General Dynamics F-16	Fighter	1976
5–10	Gruman E-2C Hawkeye	Early warning and control aircraft	1976
10	Lockheed C-5A Galaxy	Long-range transport	1975
7	Boeing 707-320C	Tanker/transport	1977
7	Boeing 707-39JC	Tanker/transport	1975
12	Boeing 747-131	Freighter/transport	1975
10	Boeing E-3A AWACS	Airborne warning and control system plane	–
4	Boeing 747-200F	Freighter	1977
3	Lockheed P-3C Orion	Anti-sub	1976
202	Bell AH-1J Sea Cobra	Gunship, helicopter	Dec. 1972
287	Bell 214A-1 (Isfahan)	Utility helicopter	Dec. 1972
39	Bell 214C	Advanced utility helicopter	1976
2	Bell 214B Big Lifter	Cargo helicopter	1975
6	Bell 214A	Utility helicopter	1977
6	Sikorsky S-G5A	Heavy-lift helicopter	1975
6	Sikorsky RH-53D	Helicopter	1975
91	Bell-Agusta 206 Jet Ranger	Helicopter	1973
6	Bell-Agusta 21P	Helicopter	1974
22	Boeing-Meridionali CH47C	Helicopter	1974
2	Sikorsky-Agusta S-G1A-4	Helicopter	1976
7	'Spruance' class 7600t	Destroyer	1974
6	'Spruance' class 7800t	Destroyer	1974
3	'Tang' class	Submarine	1975
2,500+	Hughes AGM-G54 Maverick	TV guide A–S missile	1973

Table 4.7 (continued)

Quantity[b]	Weapon designation	Weapon description	Year of order
704	Hughes ATM-54A Phoenix	A-A missile	1973, 1976
6,200	Hughes BGM-71A tow	ATM	1972–6
222	MCD-D AGM-84A Harpoon	A-S/S missile	1974
634	MCD-D FGM-77A Dragon	ATM	1975
754+	Raytheon AIM-9J Sidewinder	AAM	1974–6
516+	Raytheon AIM-7E Sparrow	AAM	1973, 1974, 1976, 1977
432	Raytheon AIM-7F Sparrow	AAM	1974
3,168	Raytheon AIM-9L Sidewinder	AAM	1974, 1975, 1976
186	Raytheon AIM-9H	AAM	1978
–	General Dynamics RIM-67A	ShShM/Sh AM	1974
–	Rockwell International AGM-53A	ASM	1974
414	Torpedo MK 46	–	1975
–	Ford M-113 A1	APC	1976
–	Raytheon MIM-23B Hawk	SAM	1977
10,000	Koll/MDD/Raytheon FGM-77A	Landmob/port	1977

Notes: [a] Compiled by the author from the sources below.
[b] Not all the items were delivered, as the revolution, the hostage crisis and the war with Iraq have affected the deliveries.
For meaning of abbreviations see pp. 155–7.
Source: SIPRI 1974–80

Table 4.8 UK–Iranian arms agreements, 1973–9

Weapon designation	Weapon description	Year of order
Chieftain MK3 and MK5	Tank	–
Chieftain MK5 (Shir Iran)	Tank	1974
Chieftain ARV	Tank	1977
Alvis Scorpion	Light tank	1975, 1976
Alvis Scorpion	Armed recon. vehicle	1973
Fox	Scout car	1976
Fox	Armoured car	1975
FV-4204	Armoured recovery vehicle	1975, 1977
FV-4205	AVLB	1977
Vickers	Armoured recovery vehicle	1976
Westland and Sea King	ASW helicopter	1974
Vosper Thorneycroft	Aircraft carrier	1977
–	Fleet replenishment	1974
–	Support ship	1974, 1977

Table 4.8 (continued)

Weapon designation	Weapon description	Year of order
Rapier M-548	SAM-tracked	1976
BAC Rapier	SAM-tracked	1974
BAC Rapier	SAM-towed	1974
BAC Rapier Blindfire and Short Tigercat	S-A Missile	1974
Sistel Seakiller I & II	S-S missile	1973
BAC Swingfire	A-T missile	1973

Note: For meaning of abbreviations see pp. 155–7.
Source: SIPRI 1974–80

Table 4.9 Iranian arms agreements with France, Soviet Union, Italy and Netherlands, 1973–9

Supplier	Weapon designation	Weapon description	Year of order
France	Dassault Falcon 20	Transport aircraft	1975
	'Kaman' class	Missile boat	1974
	AS 11/12	ASM	1973–4
	AS 12	ASM	1974
	MM.38 Exocet	ShShM	1974
	Hot	ATM	1979
Soviet Union[a]	SAM-7 and SAM-9 6000 of each	SAM	
	VCI BMP-1	APC	Nov. 1979
	ASU-85 and ZSU-23-4	SP A/T and A/Agan	
	BMP-76	Armoured car	1976
Italy	SH-30 Sea King	Helicopter	1977
	Seakiller/Marte	A Sh M	1978
	CH-47C Chinook	Helicopter	1977
Netherlands	Fokker-VFWF.27 Friendship	Transport	Feb. 1973 Sept. 1973
	F-27MK400 M and F27MK600	Transport	1976
	Kortenaer class	Frigate	1978

Notes: [a] Under $414 million.
[b] Agreement signed during War Minister Toufanian's visit to Moscow in November 1976.
Source: SIPRI 1974–80

Chapter five

The political economy of military expenditure in Iran during the war

Introduction

As noted in chapter four, during the Revolution, the Shah's militarization of Iran, and in particular the massive arms imports from the US were much criticized by the revolutionary leaders. It was promised that, if successful in toppling the Shah's regime, the revolution would reduce Iran's military expenditure (Milex) and change the country's military orientations and arms imports.

Therefore, it is not surprising to note that the revolution, after successfully deposing the old regime, had a major impact on Milex and arms imports. They were both reduced significantly, while at the same time many arms agreements with the US were cancelled.

Among them were the agreements for 160 F–16 fighters, worth $3.5 billion, seven AWACS worth $1.3 billion and 400 Phoenix missiles worth $1.6 billion. In addition, the agreement for building the Chah Bahar naval base worth $1.2 billion was cancelled, as were numerous other contracts. Many agreements with Western European countries were also terminated. Iran, for example, asked the UK to suspend or alter arms contracts, with a total value of $4.0 billion (SIPRI 1980).

The arms exporters to the Middle East, in particular those from the US and the UK, were openly complaining about the severe economic problems caused by these cancellations. For example, as noted before, during the 1973–8 period, Iran had purchased $20 billion worth of arms from the US alone. As well as these huge arms imports, Iran had also contributed towards research and development (R & D) for the production of certain arms in the US during the 1970s period.

Thus, during that period, arms sales to Iran, as well as the receipt of large sums in defence R & D, had meant that, first the US armed forces were in a position to purchase military hardware at a lower price than would have otherwise been possible, given the reduction in unit costs. Second, the US was in a position, having reduced its unit costs of arms production, to export arms elsewhere at a more competitive price than it would have been otherwise possible. Therefore, the very serious concern shown by the military industrial complex (MIC) in countries such as the US is understandable.

The seriousness of reducing Iran's Milex and arms imports can be understood better if we can imagine what would have happened if the example set by Iran had been followed by other countries in the region. This is to say that, if Iran had reduced its Milex and arms imports, then other countries in the region could not have found any justification for their own high Milex and arms imports.

Given the dependency of the MICs in industrialized economies on arms sales, it cannot be too difficult to note the probable consequences of such a rapid and sudden demilitarization of the Gulf on advanced economies. However, the Iraqi invasion of Iran put an end to the opportunity of testing this scenario.

The focus in this chapter is an attempt to demonstrate the effects of the revolution and the subsequent war on Iran's Milex and the value of arms imports. The defence and arms-imports burden will be noted, and the changes since the revolution/war will be analysed. As will be demonstrated in chapter eight, much of Iran's military imports are acquired through third parties and from the black markets. Given this, it seems an impossible task to calculate the true cost of such arms acquisitions. None the less an attempt is made in this chapter to provide the reader with an educated guess as to the value of arms imports since the revolution.

Since the downfall of the Shah, there have been many changes in military manpower and its composition. Therefore these, as well as changes in major weapon systems held by the Iranian armed forces before and after the revolution, will form a further part of study in this chapter.

The impact of the war on Milex and defence burden

The figures for Milex and the measurement of defence burden during the 1979–85 period are provided in table 5.1. The GDP/Milex figures during the 1973–85 period (selected years) are graphically presented in figure 5.1. In 1979, as can be seen, Milex was 278 billion rials, representing a massive reduction of over 60 per cent on the 1978 expenditure (see table 4.1). Therefore, in 1979, namely the first year of the revolution, the defence burden was 4.5 per cent representing a rapid decline since the fall of the Shah, as the corresponding figure for 1978 was 14.1 per cent.

Table 5.1 Ratio of military expenditures (Milex) in GDP (oil including and excluding) – defence burden,* Iran, 1979–85

	Milex	GDP (including oil)	Share of defence in GDP (%)	GDP (excluding oil)	Share of defence in GDP (%)	
1979	278	6053	4.5	4377	6.4	
1980	317	6759	4.7	5778	5.5	
1981	1,007	8218	12.3	7288	13.8	
1982	1,300	10,621	12.3	8852	14.7	Average annual growth of Milex – 1979–85 (%)* 29.2
1983	1,500	13,471	11.1	11,662	12.9	
1984	1,853	15,030	12.3	12,926[b]	14.0	
1985	1,295	15,306	8.5	13,163[b]	9.2	
Average share for year*			9.3		10.9	

Notes: [a] Author's calculations. The figures quoted for Milex and GDP are in current billion rials.
[b] Estimated by the author.
Sources: IISS 1980/1 to 1986/7; Central Bank of Iran, Annual Report and Balance Sheet, 1358, 1362; IMFa November 1986

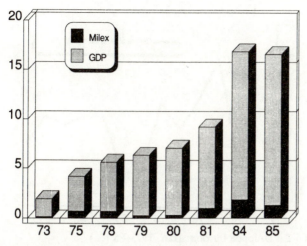

Figure 5.1 GDP and military expenditures (Milex): Iran, 1973–85 (selected years)
Source: Based on Mofid 1987: 181, table 5.2; IISS 1980/1–1986/7; Central Bank of Iran: 1358, 1362; IMFa, November 1986

Between 1979 and 1980 Milex was raised by 14 per cent, where it increased to 317 billion rials.

Therefore we can with certainty claim that the revolution, as it had promised, in the first two years of its existence, successfully reduced the amount of Milex and had lowered the defence burden in Iran.

However, such a major achievement was stopped when, in September 1980, the Iraqis invaded Iran. This attack put an end to the revolutionary regime's policy of keeping Milex low, as it had managed to do directly after the revolution.

As can be seen in table 5.1, Iran's Milex increased by 218 per cent between 1980 and 1981, rising from 317 billion rials to 1,007 billion rials. In all, during the period under study, Milex has increased by an average annual growth rate of 29.2 per cent, representing an average defence burden of 9.3 per cent in GDP (including oil).

The corresponding figures for the pre-revolution period of 1973–8 were 37 and 13 per cent respectively. Thus it can be seen that, since the revolution, there has been a decline both in the average annual growth of Milex and in the defence burden.

However, if the corresponding figures of the pre- and post-war periods are compared, it can be noted that indeed there has been a massive increase in Milex and the defence burden since the war.

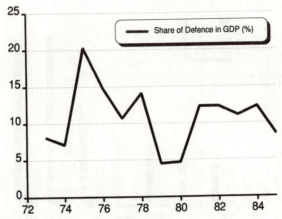

Figure 5.2   Defence burden: Iran, 1973–85 (%)
Sources: Based on Mofid 1987: 181, table 5.2; IISS 1980/1–1986/7;
Central Bank of Iran: 1358, 1362; IMFa, November 1986

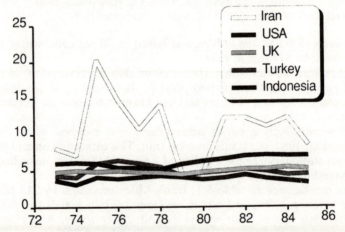

Figure 5.3   Defence burden: Iran, USA, UK, Turkey and Indonesia,
1973–85 (%)
Sources: Based on Mofid 1987: 181, table 5.2; IISS 1980/1–1986/7;
Central Bank of Iran: 1358, 1362; IMFa, November 1986

This can best be seen in figure 5.2 where the pre- and post-war
defence-burden ratios are graphically illustrated.

The defence-burden figures of selected countries during the
1979–85 period are given in table 5.2. As can be seen, in 1979, for
the first time, Iran's defence burden was more or less comparable

with the countries outlined in the table. All except the USA and
Greece were spending 4.5 per cent or less of their GDPs on Milex.
In figure 5.3, Iran's defence burden during the 1973–85 period has
been compared to those of the USA, UK, Turkey and Indonesia.
The figure speaks for itself and, as can be seen, Iran by far has had
a much higher defence burden than all other countries.

Moreover, while the defence burden for many countries, as
shown in table 5.2, has remained more or less the same during the
period under study, Iran's defence burden since the war has
increased rapidly (see figure 5.3).

Table 5.2 World military expenditure (Milex) as percentage of GDP*,
selected countries, 1979–85

	1979	1980	1981	1982	1983	1984	1985
Canada	1.9	1.8	1.9	2.0	2.1	2.2	2.2
USA	5.9	6.3	6.6	7.0	7.1	7.0	7.0
Belgium	3.3	3.3	3.5	3.3	3.3	3.1	3.0
Denmark	2.3	2.4	2.5	2.5	2.5	2.3	2.2
France	3.9	4.0	4.2	4.1	4.2	4.1	4.1
FR Germany	3.3	3.3	3.4	3.4	3.4	3.3	3.2
Greece	6.3	5.7	7.0	6.9	6.3	7.2	7.1
Italy	2.4	2.4	2.5	2.6	2.7	2.7	2.7
Turkey	4.3	4.7	4.9	5.2	4.9	4.4	4.5
UK	4.5	4.8	5.0	5.2	5.2	5.4	5.2
India	3.5	3.6	3.8	3.9	3.9	3.9	4.0
Pakistan	4.7	4.7	5.1	5.5	5.4	(5.5)	(5.4)
Indonesia	(4.1)	(3.8)	(4.0)	(4.4)	(3.9)	(3.6)	(3.3)
Japan	0.9	0.9	0.9	0.9	1.0	1.0	1.0
Australia	2.6	2.7	2.7	2.9	3.0	3.0	3.2

Notes: * GDP at current market prices.
       ( ) Uncertain data.
Source: SIPRI 1987: table 6A3

The impact of the war on the value of arms imports and on the arms-imports burden

Table 5.3 provides figures of estimated arms imports as well as the
estimation of arms-imports burden during the 1979–85 period. The
graphical presentation of arms-imports burden during the whole of
the 1973–85 period is shown in figure 5.4. As can be noted, given
the rapid decline in Milex soon after the revolution, the arms
imports were also correspondingly reduced. The value of arms
imports fell by 67 per cent, from 416 billion rials in 1978 (see table
4.4) to 139 billion rials in 1979. The corresponding rise between

1979 and 1980 was 14.4 per cent, where it increased to 159 billion rials, representing an arms-imports burden of 16.8 and 15.6 per cent respectively during the same two years.

Table 5.3 Ratio of arms imports in total imports (burden of arms imports),[a] Iran, 1979–85

	Arms imports[b] A	Non-military imports B	Total imports A + B	Ratio of arms imports to total imports[a] (%) A/(A+B)
1979	139	686	825	16.8
1980	159	863	1,022	15.6
1981	504	985	1,489	33.8
1982	650	1,185	1,835	35.4
1983	750	1,583	2,333	32.1
1984	927	1,328	2,255	41.1
1985	648	1,061	1,709	37.9

Average annual growth of military-imports[a] 1979–85: 29.2%

	1979–80	1979–85	1981–5
Burden of arms imports, average per year	16.2	30.4	36.1

Notes: [a] Author's calculation. The figures quoted for defence and non-defence imports are in current billion rials.
[b] Military-related imports have been estimated at 50 per cent of total military expenditure for each year. These have been calculated under the assumption that, unlike the Shah's period, no major advanced military items have been received. Most of the imports are spare parts, small arms and ammunition. The imports of 'major weapons' have been those of the 'second best' and not those of the most expensive types. However, most of the imports have come via black market and third parties, and this should have increased their costs significantly. In consideration of all these factors, our estimation of military-related imports has been based on 50 per cent of the total military expenditures for each year, as opposed to 60 per cent for 1973–8. We, however, admit that this is only an educated guess.

Sources: IMFa 1985; and IISS 1980/1 to 1986/7

However, as a result of the invasion and the subsequent increase in Milex, arms imports were also increased significantly. They increased to 217 billion rials in 1980 and 504 billion rials in 1981, representing an increase of 217 and 132 per cent respectively.

In all, during 1979–85, arms imports increased by 29.2 per cent on average each year, a substantial rate of increase by any standard. However, the fact that, since the revolution, no major advanced military items have been received and that most of the supplies are of the 'cheaper' and 'second-best' varieties, has meant that there has been a reduction in the annual average growth rate of military imports. For example, during the 1973–8 period (a

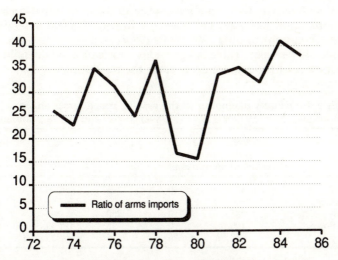

Figure 5.4 Arms–import burden: Iran, 1973–85 (%)
Sources: Based on SIPRI 1980: 96–7, tables 3.6 and 3.7; IMFa 1985: IISS 1980/1–1986/7

period of massive militarization), arms imports had increased by 37 per cent on average each year.

None the less it should be underlined that, since the invasion, there has been a massive increase in the arms-imports burden. This burden during 1979 and 1980 on average each year was 16.2 per cent, rising to 36.1 per cent between 1981 and 1985. Therefore, if the pre-war (i.e. 1973–80) and post-war (1981–5) defence burdens are compared, it can be seen that there has been a significant increase in such a burden. The corresponding figures for the arms-imports burden during the same period are 26.1 and 36.1 per cent respectively (see further figure 5.4).

In conclusion, it can be said that one of the major consequences of the war on Iran has been the inability of the revolutionary regime to keep the Milex and arms imports low, as they had just done in the first two years of the revolution before Iran was invaded.

The impact of the revolution and the war on military manpower and its composition, as well as on the quality and quantity of major weapon systems held in Iran

The revolution, as noted in chapter two, had a major impact on the armed forces. Many high-ranking officers were either purged or executed. The total number of men in the three forces (army, air force and the navy) fell from the high of 415,000 in 1979/80 (pre-revolution) to only 240,000 in 1980/1, representing a decline of over 42 per cent. Table 5.4 provides information on the military manpower of the regular army since the revolution.

Table 5.4 Military manpower of the regular armed forces and its composition, Iran, 1979/80, 1980/1, 1984/5, 1986/7 and 1987/8 (thousands)

	1979/80 (pre-Revolution)	*1980/1 (post-Revolution)*	*1984/5*	*1986/7*	*1987/8*
Total	415	240	305	355	355
of which:					
Army	285	150	250	305	305
Air Force	100	70	35	35	35
Navy	30	20	15	15	15

Sources: IISS 1979/80 to 1987/88

It can be seen that, given the initial near disintegration of the forces soon after the revolution, even by 1987/8, they had not regained their pre-revolution strength. The total manpower of the regular armed forces has increased to 355,000, which is still 14.5 per cent less than what it was in 1979/80.

A major impact on the armed forces since the revolution, however, has been a parallel rise and a rapid development of the Revolutionary Guard Corps (RGC) or *Pasdaran-e Enqelab*. From a modest beginning in 1979/80 to protect the revolution, they now have become a major force not only in protecting the revolution, but also since the Iraqi invasion in defending the country.

By 1986/7 the RGCs had formed themselves into different branches, consisting of ground forces, naval forces, marines and air forces. It is estimated that by 1986 there were some 300,000 volunteers in ground forces, with 11 regional commands. Their artillery included surface-to-surface missiles (SSM) and air defences. They serve independently or with the regular army. They also control *Basij* (see below).

The strength (i.e. the number of men under arms) of the Revolutionary Guards' Naval Forces is not clearly known. They have, however, five island bases, namely Al Farsiyah, Halul (oil platfrom), Sirri, Abu Musa and Lark. These forces have some 40 Swedish Boghamma fast boats armed with anti-tank guided weapons (ATGW); recoilless launchers (RCL) and machine guns.

The coast-defence elements' artillery includes some Ch HY-2

missiles, better known as *silkworm* SSM, in at least three of their sites. It is also believed that they might have Italian SSM in their possession. The marine corps is reported to include some three brigades. Not much has been reported on their activities at this stage.

The Revolutionary Guards' air forces have gone through much improvement in the last couple of years. They now have an important role in the air defence of major installations. It is estimated that in 1986, they had at least 22 F-6 fighter planes.

As well as the establishment of the RGCs, in 1981 the Youth Brigades (Basij) was also formed. It is believed that by 1986/7, as many as 1 million were in Basij Forces.[1]

Therefore, in all, since the revolution, there has been an increase of at least 310 per cent (excluding women under arms) in the number of people under arms, as by 1987 their number had increased to 1,700,000.

Table 5.5 illustrates the list of major weapon systems held by the regular armed forces for selected years since the revolution. If the quality and quantity of these weapons are compared with those of the pre-revolution period, some major changes can be observed.

Table 5.5 Major weapon systems held by the regular armed forces, Iran, 1979/80, 1980/1, 1984/5 and 1987/8.

	1979/80 *(last year of the Shah)*	*1980/1* *(first year of the Revolution)*	*1984/5[a]*	*1987/8[a]*
Tanks	1,985	1,985	1,050(?)	1,310(?)[b]
Combat Aircraft	445	445	95(?)	60(?)[c]
Helicopters	684	684	320(?)	300(?)[d]
Armoured fighting vehicles	825	825	1,190	1,060

Notes: [a] Losses and incomplete reporting of resupply make it impossible to estimate true numbers.
[b] Among them: perhaps 1,000 T-54/-55; 250 T-59, T-62, T-72 (all Russian and East European-supplied, many captured from the Iraqis), and a very small number of Chieftain, M-47/-48, and M-60AI. Therefore, since the war, near total losses in pre-war tank holdings and major changes in types and supplies of tanks.
[c] Still pre-revolution/-war holdings. No new supplies of any significance.
[d] Same as [c].
(?) Questionable if all operational.
Sources: IISS 1979/80 to 1987/88

As noted in chapter four, during the 1973–8 period, the US was by far the biggest supplier of the most advanced weapons to Iran. It was also noted that, by 1979/80, Iran had received 445 combat aircraft, among them 190 F-4s and 166 F-5s. There were also 1,985 tanks delivered to Iran; among them were 875 Chieftains and 250 Scorpions.

However, given the revolution and the subsequent embargoes against direct arms sales to Iran, as well as losses due to the war, by 1987/8 there were only some 1,310 tanks, 60 combat aircraft and 300 helicopters held by the armed forces.

Since the revolution and the war the most important change in Iran's armoury has been in the tank division. Most of the advanced British-made Chieftain and Scorpion tanks have been destroyed. The new tanks are mainly all Russian/Eastern European made, amongst them are 1,000 T-54/55s and 250 T-59s. Therefore, as shown in table 5.5, since the war, not only has the quality of the tanks held been totally changed, but also, as far as quantity is concerned, in 1987 Iran had 675 tanks less than what it had in 1980.

As for the combat aircraft and helicopters, no new major systems have been supplied since the revolution. However, due to losses incurred since the war, their actual numbers have been reduced significantly, from 445 and 684 in 1980 to 60 and 300 in 1987 respectively. Futhermore, it is believed that, due to parts shortages and other technical problems, not all of the above are operational anyway.

As it appears, it can therefore be said that, since the war, there has been a near collapse in the availability of advanced major weaponry systems held by the armed forces in Iran. Therefore it seems safe to conclude that the very large sums that Iran has been spending on arms imports has been mainly on spare parts, 'second-rated' weapons, as well as shells, mines and missiles, amongst others.

None the less high expenditures have been necessary since arms prices have been much inflated, given that most have been acquired through third parties and black markets, a point to which we will return in chapter eight.

Conclusion

In this chapter it was demonstrated that the revolutionary leaders, in the first two years of their existence and prior to the Iraqi invasion, rapidly and significantly reduced Iran's Milex and arms imports. However, this major post-revolutionary achievement was abruptly ended when the country was attacked.

Since that time Milex and arms imports, as well as corresponding defence and arms-imports burdens, have all been increased significantly.

It was also noted that, since the war, there has been a massive rise in the number of people under arms in Iran. We observed that, while there has been a major reduction in the importance of the regular armed forces, there has been a parallel rise in importance and functions of the Revolutionary Guards.

It was also demonstrated that there has been a major change in quality and quantity of major weaponry systems held in Iran. We noted that there has been no new delivery of advanced fighter planes and helicopters. We established the fact that their numbers have been reduced significantly and, due to technical problems, not all the available stock is fully operational.

We noted that, since the revolution/war, the most important change in Iran's armoury has been in the tank division. There has been a total change in their quality and quantity during the period under study.

In all, it can be said that one of the most damaging consequences of the war has been the inability of the revolutionary leadership to keep the Milex, the arms imports and their corresponding burdens low, as they had managed to do immediately after the revolution and prior to the invasion.

Chapter six

Militarization of Iraq 1973–8: an economic analysis

Introduction

In chapter four some aspects of the militarization of Iran under the late Shah, during the 1973–8 period, were noted. The Shah's drive for regional hegemony through increases in Milex and a massive arms imports programme did not fail to have an impact on Iraq, which had its own aspirations towards its own regional role.

The reasons for and the style in which both countries pursued their militarization policies are varied and complex. Given the scope of this chapter, no attempt is made here to discuss and analyse the differences. However, the reader interested in these issues is encouraged to refer to Karsh 1987, Helms 1984, Brown and Snyder 1985, Abdulghani 1984, King 1987 and Litwak 1981, amongst others.

Therefore, what we intend to do, in this chapter is to provide an economic balance sheet of Iraq's militarization, similar in style and scope to that which was provided for Iran in chapter four.

The estimation of defence and arms-imports burdens

The figures for Milex and defence burdens during the 1973–8 period are given in table 6.1. As can be seen, Milex increased from 0.165 billion dinars in 1973 to 0.586 billion dinars in 1978, representing an average annual increase of 29 per cent.

An intersting observation to be seen in this table is that, while the military expenditure during the period under study had increased significantly, it had not increased at the rate at which GDP had grown. This is so, as the share of defence in GDP (including oil) had fallen from 10.3 to 8.4 per cent between 1973 and 1978. This is in contrast to Iran's experience during the same period. As was noted in chapter four, Iran's defence burden had increased from 8.1 per cent in 1973 to 14.1 per cent in 1978.

Table 6.1 Ratio of military expenditure (Milex) in GDP (oil including and excluding) – defence burden[a], Iraq, 1973–8

	Milex	GDP Share of defence (including oil)[b]	in GDP[a]	GDP Share of defence (excluding oil)[b]	in GDP[a]
1973	0.165	1.6	10.3	0.65	25.4
1974	0.236	3.4	6.9	1.3	18.1
1975	0.356	4.0	8.9	1.6	22.2
1976	0.394	5.2	7.6	2.1	18.8
1977	0.492	5.9	8.3	2.3	21.4
1978	0.586	7.0	8.4	2.8	21.0

Average annual growth of Milex 1973–8:[a] 29.0%

Notes: [a] Author's calculation. The figures quoted for Milex and GDP are in current billion Iraqi dinars.
   [b] Calculated by the author, based on the information in EIU 1980.
Sources: United Nations Economic and Social Commission for Western Asia 1981; IMFa 1986; IISS 1973/4; and EIU 1980

Furthermore, Iran's Milex had increased by 37 per cent on average each year, while, as was noted, the corresponding figure for Iraq is 29 per cent.

At this point, if we compare Iraq's defence burden figures with those of other selected countries whose figures were given in chapter four, table 4.2, we can note that, Iraq, like Iran, during the period under observation, had allocated a much larger share of its GDP to defence than any other country mentioned in that table.

This observation once more reinforces the relationship that exists between oil revenues on the one hand and high levels of Milex on the other.

Table 6.2 provides data on the estimated value of Iraq's arms imports, as well as the ratio of arms imports to total imports during the 1973–8 period. As can be noted, the value of arms imports increased from 0.058 billion dinars in 1973 to 0.205 billion dinars in 1978, representing an average annual growth of 29 per cent.

As for the arms-import burden, it can be seen that, like the defence-burden figures, the ratio had declined from 17.8 per cent in 1973 to 14.4 per cent in 1978. Once again, this is in contrast to Iran's experience, where, as noted in chapter four, these ratios had increased significantly.

However, although the sums spent on arms imports were much less than what Iran had spent, none the less, in absolute terms, they represent a significant expenditure. Therefore, as in the study which was provided in chapter four for Iran, it is very interesting to note what Iraq had received in exchange for such impressive

Table 6.2   Ratio of arms imports in total imports – burden of arms imports[a], Iraq, 1973–8

	Arms imports[b] A	Non-military imports B	Total imports (A) + (B)	Ratio of arms imports to total imports (%)[a] A (A) + (B)
1973	0.058	0.268	0.326	17.8
1974	0.083	0.688	0.771	10.8
1975	0.123	1.22	1.343	9.1
1976	0.138	1.13	1.268	10.9
1977	0.172	1.3	1.472	11.7
1978	0.205	1.22	1.425	14.4

Average annual growth of military imports[a] 1973–8: 29.0%
Burden of arms – imports average per/year 1973–8[a] 12.4%

Notes: [a] Author's calculation. The figures quoted for defence and non-defence imports are in current billion Iraqi dinars.
[b] Military related imports have been estimated at 35 per cent of the total military expenditures for each year under observation in this table, based on the information given in the US 1972–82.
Sources: IMFa 1985; SIPRI, 1974 to 1979; IISS, 1973–4 to 1980/1; and USACDA 1984

payments. First, the confirmed arms suppliers to Iraq during the period under study will be noted.

As can be seen in table 6.5 at the end of this chapter, the Soviet Union was the major arms supplier. Indeed, if we refer to table 4.3, it can be seen that the Soviet Union had supplied 85 per cent of Iraq's total arms imports during the period under study. Different types of MiG fighter planes, helicopters, air transport tankers, heavy and light tanks, armoured carriers, and many different types of missiles were supplied by the Soviet Union. France was the next major supplier of modern weapons to Iraq.

The numbers and types of major weapon systems held by the Iraqi armed forces between 1972/3 and 1979/80 are illustrated in table 6.3. As can be seen the number of tanks, combat aircraft, helicopters and armoured fighting vehicles increased from 925, 189, 46 and 360 to 1,900, 339, 231 and 1,500 during the same period. This table shows that the great majority of the weapons supplied to Iraq were Russian made.

This, as well as our observations in chapter four, clearly demonstrates the fact that the main beneficiaries of the arms build-up in the Persian Gulf are the superpowers as well as the 'mini' and 'second-rated' powers in Europe.

Table 6.2 gave figures of the estimated value of arms imports in current billions of Iraqi dinars. Given the exchange rates,[1] the total estimated value of arms imports in $US (current prices)

Table 6.3   Major weapon systems held by the armed forces, Iraq, 1972/3–1979/80

	1972/3	*1979/80*
Tanks	925	1,900[a]
Combat aircraft	189	339[b]
Helicopters	46	231[c]
Armoured fighting vehicles	360	1,500

Notes: [a] Among them: 1700 T-54/-55/-62 and 100 T-34 medium tanks (Russian supplied).
   [b] Among them: 12TU-22; 80 MIG-23B; and 115 MIG-21 (Russian supplied).
   [c] Among them: 35 Mi-4, 14 Mi-6, and 80 Mi-8 (Russian supplied).
Sources: IISS 1972/3 and 1979/80

during the 1973–8 period is the sum of $2.7 billion. If we refer to chapter four, it can be noted that this sum was indeed much less than Iran's total military imports, which were $25.7 billion during the same period.

As mentioned before, the Soviet Union had supplied 85 per cent of Iraq's total arms imports. Therefore, the total Soviet arms sales to Iraq during the period under study was the sum of $2.2 billion.

At this point the military manpower and its composition during 1972/3 to 1979/80 will be noted. As can be seen in table 6.4, the total military manpower increased by 137 per cent from 102,000 to 222,000 during the same period. The army increased its numbers from 90,000 to 190,000, while the corresponding figures for the air force were 10,000 increasing to 28,000 during the same period.

Table 6.4   Military manpower and its composition, Iraq, 1972/3–1979/80 (thousands)

	1972/3	*Change** %	*1979/80*
Total military manpower	102	137	222
of which:			
Army	90	122	190
Air force	10	280	28
Navy	2	100	4

Note: * Author's calculation.
Sources: IISS, 1972/3 and 1979/80

The growth of the Iraqi armed forces was not as balanced as that of Iran's. The Iraqi navy did not develop to the same degree as the other branches of the armed forces. This was mainly due to Iraq's geographical limitations, as the country is virtually land-locked with a Gulf coastline of only 10 miles compared with 1,243 miles for Iran.

Conclusion

In this chapter we looked at some economic aspects of the Milex and arms imports of Iraq during the 1973–8 period. We noted that military expenditures and military imports had increased by 29 per cent on average each year during the period under study. We showed that the Soviet Union was by far the main supplier of major weapons to Iraq.

It was shown that Iraq, in contrast to Iran, had not gone for a military build-up at the break-neck speed which by 1978 had produced fatal flaws in Iran. We noted that, again in contrast to the Iranian experience, both defence- and arms-imports-burden ratios had fallen in Iraq during the period under study.

None the less, in absolute terms, Iraq had spent significant sums of money to modernize and improve its armed forces. The total number of men under arms had increased by 137 per cent, from 102,000 in 1972/3 to 222,000 in 1979/80. The focus during this period was on the expansion of ground forces where their numbers increased from 90,000 to 190,000 during the same period. We also demonstrated that by the end of the period under observation, Iraq had received an impressive assortment of weapons, mainly from the Soviet Union.

In all, it should be noted that, by adopting a 'less big', as opposed to 'big-push' strategy of development and modernization, both in the civilian and military sectors, Iraq, by the end of the 1978/9 period was in an enviable position, a far cry from the situation which Iran had pushed itself into.

Table 6.5 Confirmed arms suppliers to Iraq, 1973–8

Supplier	Weapon designation	Weapon description	Year of order
Soviet Union	MIG-21	Fighter	1973
	Mi-6	Helicopter	1973
Czechoslovakia	Aero L-392	Trainer/Strike	1973
France	Aerospatiale A Covette II	Helicopter	1974
	Aerospatiale SS-11	A-T missile	1974
Soviet Union	MIG-23 'Flogger'	Fighter	1973
	Sukhoi-20	Aircraft	1973
	SS-N-2 'Styx'	Naval S-S missile	1973
	Fast attach missile boat	Displ: 165T	1973
	AA-2-p2 Atoll	AAM	1973
	'Scud'	SSM	1974
	T-55/T-62	Main battle tank	1973
		Self propelled gun	1973
UK	HS Hawk	Fighter	
France	Aerospatiale A Covette III	Helicopter	1974

Table 6.5 (continued)

Supplier	Weapon designation	Weapon description	Year of order
	Dassault Falcon	Transport	1975
	Dassault Mirage F-1	Fighter	1975
	Aerospatiale SA-321	Helicopter	1976
	Dassault Mirage F-1	Fighter	1976
	Aerospatiale AS-11/12	ASM	1974
France/UK	Aerospatiale/Westland SA-342	Helicopter	1976
	Dassault-Bregeut BAC Jagnan	Fighter	1976
USA	Lockheed C-130 Hercules	Transport Aircraft	1976
Soviet Union	'Scud'	SSM	1975
	–	ATM	1975
	T-64	Tank	1975
		152-mm SP rapid fire	1975
	Mil Mi-8	Helicopter	1975
	Mil-Mi-24	Helicopter	1975
France	AM-39 Exocet	ASM	1976
	AMX-10P	Armoured Car	1977
	AMX-30	MBT	1977
	Mirage F1C	Fighter	1977
	HOT	ATM	1976
	R-550 Magic	AAM	1976
	SA-321G Super Ferlon	Helicopter	1977
France/UK	SA-330 Puma	LOT	1976
Switzerland	MBB-223 K Flamingo	Trainer	1977
Soviet Union	AA-2 Attol	AAM	1976
	AN-12	Transport	1976
	AN-24	Transport	1976
	Mig-23	Fighter	1976
	Osa	Missile Patrol boat	1976
	SA-6	SAM	1977
	SSB-2 Styx	ShShM	1976
	T-62	MBT	1976
	An-Civil	Transport	1976
	1/1-76 Candid	Transport	1978
	Mi-10 Hawke	Helicopter	1978
	MIG-23S	Fighter	1976
	SA-6 Gainful	SAM	1976
	Osa-2 Class	FPB	1976
Switzerland	AS-202 Brarto	Trainer	1978
France	Mirage F-1B	Trainer	1977
	AM-39 Exocet	ASM	1978
	Crotale	SAM	1976

Sources: SIPRI 1972/3 to 1979
For meaning of abbreviations see pp. 155–7

Chapter seven

The political economy of military expenditure in Iraq during the war

Introduction

In chapter six some aspects of the militarization of Iraq during the 1973–8 period were noted. It was shown that Iraq, in contrast to Iran, had not gone for a military build-up at break neck speed. Indeed, we demonstrated that both the defence- and arms-imports burden ratios had fallen during this period. This was so, as military expenditure (Milex) had not increased as fast as the GDP in the period under consideration.

However, it was noted that in absolute terms significant sums of money had been spent on modernization and the improvement of Iraq's armed forces. It was also shown that during that period the Soviet Union was by far the largest supplier of advanced weapons to Iraq.

Since the Iraqi invasion of Iran in September 1980, there has been a significant change in Iraq's militarization, in terms of the value of Milex/arms imports, the number of people under arms and the quantity of military equipment held by the armed forces.

Therefore the focus of this chapter is an attempt to demonstrate the effects of the war on Iraq's Milex and arms imports. The defence- and arms-imports-burden ratios will be noted, and changes since the invasion will be analysed. Then the changes in military manpower, as well as the changes in major weapon systems held by the Iraqi forces before and since the war, will be the subject of study.

The impact of the war on Milex and the defence burden

The figures of Milex and the measurement of the defence burden during the 1979–85 period are provided in table 7.1. The GDP/Milex figures during the 1973–85 period (selected years) are graphically illustrated in figure 7.1. As can be seen, in 1979, Milex was 0.789 billion dinars, representing a defence burden of 7 per cent in GDP (including oil). By 1980, while GDP (including oil) had increased by 41 per cent, Milex had been raised by only 11.4 per cent. Given this, therefore, the defence burden for the same year had actually fallen to 5.6 per cent.

Table 7.1 Ratio of military expenditure (Milex) in GDP (oil including and excluding) – defence burden*, Iraq, 1979–85

	Milex	GDP (including oil)	Share of defence in GDP*	GDP (excluding oil)	Share of defence in GDP*
1979	0.789	11.4	7.0	5.0	16.0
1980	0.879	15.8	5.6	6.0	14.6
1981	1.4	11.1	12.6	7.9	17.7
1982	2.4	12.6	19.0	5.1	47.1
1983	3.2	13.1	24.4	6.6	48.5
1984	4.3	13.9	31.0	7.6	57.0
1985	4.0	16.6	24.0	10.8	37.0
Average defence burden:					
1979–85			17.6		34.0
1973–9			8.2		20.4

Average annual growth of Milex 1979–85: 31%

Notes: * Author's calculation. The figures quoted for Milex and GDP are in current billion Iraqi dinars.
Sources: IISS 1979/80 to 1986/7; OPEC 1985; Republic of Iraq, 1983 and United Nations Economic and Statistical Commission for Western Asia, 1986

Then came the invasion of Iran in September 1980. In 1981, GDP (including oil) fell by 30 per cent to 11.1 billion dinars, while at the same time Milex increased by 59 per cent to 1.4 billion dinars. As a result of this rapid increase in Milex, accompanied by a significant decrease in GDP, the corresponding defence burden increased to 12.6 per cent in the same year.

In all, during the period of 1979 to 1985, there was an unparalleled rise in Milex on the one hand, followed by a massive fall in GDP on the other (see figure 7.1). Given this, there has been a significant increase in the defence burden, which has amounted to 17.6 per cent on average each year of GDP (including oil), a rapid rate of increase by any standards, including Iraq's own pre-war standards. During the 1973–9 period, the average annual defence burden was 8.2 per cent. Therefore it can safely be argued that, as a result of the war, there has been a rapid increase in Milex, while at the same time GDP has been falling significantly, resulting in a massive rise in the defence burden. This can best be seen in figure

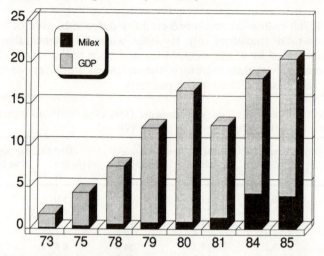

Figure 7.1 GDP and military expenditures (Milex): Iraq, 1973–85
(selected years) (billion Iraqi dinars)
Sources: United Nations Economic and Social Commission for Western
Asia 1981, 1986; IMFa 1986; IISS 1973/4, 1979/80–1986/7; EIU 1980;
OPEC 1985; Republic of Iraq 1983

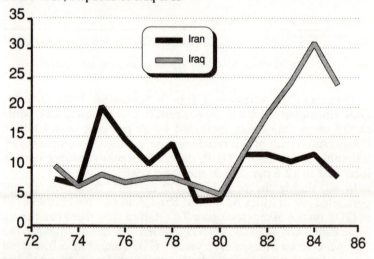

Figure 7.2 Defence burden: Iran and Iraq, 1973–85 (%)
Sources: United Nations Economic and Social Commission for Western
Asia 1981, 1986; IMFa 1986, November; IISS 1973/4, 1979/80–1986/7;
EIU 1980; OPEC 1985; Republic of Iraq 1983; IISS 1980/1–1986/7;
Central Bank of Iran: 1358, 1362

7.2, a graphical presentation of Iraq's defence burden (1973–85). For the purpose of comparison, Iran's defence burden during the same period is also illustrated.

As noted in chapter six, while in pre-war Iraq Milex had increased, the rate of growth had always been far less than the rate at which GDP had grown. Thus another major consequence of the war, as far as Iraq is concerned, is a departure from past policies.

The impact of the war on the value of arms imports and the arms-imports burden

At the outset it should be emphasized that, as with Iran, a wall of secrecy surrounds Iraq's arms imports, especially when different countries have been financing its imports (see chapter ten). Therefore it seems an impossible task to try to calculate the true cost of such imports. However, in this chapter we have attempted to provide an educated guess on the value of arms imports since the war.

Table 7.2 provides figures of estimated arms imports, as well as an estimation of the imports burden during the period under study. As can be seen, the value of arms imports in 1979 was the

Table 7.2 Ratio of arms imports in total imports – burden of arms imports[a] Iraq, 1979–85

	Arms imports[b]	Non-military imports	Total imports	Ratio of arms imports to total imports[a](%)
	A	B	A + B	
1979	0.484	2.6	3.08	15.7
1980	0.539	4.1	4.64	11.6
1981	0.858	6.1	6.96	12.3
1982	1.47	6.3	7.77	18.9
1983	1.96	3.8	5.76	34.0
1984	3.00	3.5	6.5	46.1
1985	2.8	3.3	6.1	45.9

Average annual growth rate of military-inputs[a] 1979–85: 34.0%
Burden of arms imports average for year, 1979–85[a] 27.0%

Notes: [a] Author's calculation. The figures quoted for defence and non-defence imports are current billion Iraqi dinars.
[b] Military-related imports have been estimated at 61.3 per cent of total military expenditures for each year during the 1979–83 period. This estimation has been based on the information given in US 1985. For the years 1984 and 1985, the military-related imports have been calculated at 70 per cent of the total military expenditures. This is based on the information provided in SIPRI (see sources below) concerning large-scale military agreements signed in 1984/5 between Iraq, the Soviet Union and France. We, however, admit that this is only an educated guess.
Sources: IMFa 1985; SIPRI 1984, 1985, 1986; US ACDA 1985; and IISS 1979/80 to 1986/7

sum of 0.484 billion dinars, rising by 11.4 per cent to 0.539 in 1980. Then, as a result of the invasion, it increased by 59.2 per cent to 0.858 billion dinars in 1981. However, as noted in chapter three, during this period there was a massive increase in non-military imports. Given this, the ratio of arms-imports burden fell from 15.7 per cent in 1979 to 11.6 per cent in 1980 and 12.3 per cent in 1981, while rising to 18.9 per cent in 1982.

However, since 1983, as can be seen, there has been a massive increase in arms imports (mostly due to increased arms deliveries from the Soviet Union), accompanied by a rapid decline in civilian imports. Thus the arms-imports-burden ratio increased to 34 per cent (1983), 46.1 per cent (1984) and 45.9 per cent (1985). These can best be seen in figure 7.3, where Iraq's arms-import burden during the 1973–85 period is illustrated. For the purpose of comparison, Iran's arms-imports burden is also shown.

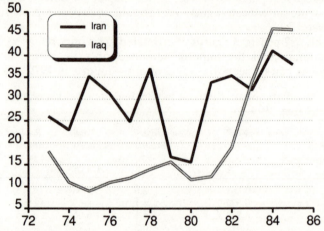

Figure 7.3 Arms–import burden: Iran and Iraq, 1973–85 (%)
Sources: Based on Mofid 1987: 181, table 5.2; IISS 1979/80 to 1986/7; Central Bank of Iran: 1358, 1362; IMFa 1985, November 1986; SIPRI 1984–6; USACDA 1985

The impact of the war on military manpower, its composition, as well as on the quality and quantity of major weapon systems held by Iraq

Table 7.3 provides information on the Iraqi armed forces during the 1979/80 to 1987/8 period. As can be seen, there has been a huge increase in the number of people involved, one way or another, with the armed forces since the war. As shown in the table, the total military manpower in 1979/80 was 222,000, rising by 9 per cent to 242,000 in 1980/1. Then, as a result of the invasion and the continuing war, by 1984/5 the figure had increased by 166 per cent (1980/1 = base) to 643,000, rising by 31.4 per cent to 845,000 in 1986/7. By 1987/8 it had risen to the grand total of 1,000,000.

Table 7.3 Military manpower and its composition: Iraq, 1979/80, 1980/1, 1984/5, 1986/7 and 1987/8 (thousands)

	1979/80	*1980/1*	*1984/5*	*1986/7*	*1987/8*
Total	222	242	643	845	1,000
of which:					
Army	190[a]	200	600	800	955[b]
Air force	28	38	38	40	40
Navy	4	4	5	5	5

Notes: [a] Excluding around 250,000 reserves.
[b] Including around 480,000 active reserves. Furthermore, while in 1979/80 there were 750,000 in the People's Army (a paramilitary force), this number has increased to 650,000 in 1987/8.
Sources: IISS, 1979/80 to 1987/8

In all, the total military manpower has increased by 350 per cent during the same period, a massive rate of increase, even compared with Iraq's own rate of militarization before the war. In 1972/3 to 1979/80, the total military manpower figure had increased by 137 per cent (see table 6.4).

This, indeed, is a massive rate of militarization of a country in terms of the percentage of the population under arms. In 1979/80, only 1.7 per cent of the total population was in the forces, while the corresponding figure for 1987/8 has *massively* increased to 17 per cent of the total. If the above figure is compared with Iran's it can be noted that, given Iran's much larger population, only 3.6 per cent of the total population were, one way or another, in the forces in the same year. Thus it can be seen that the war has had a much bigger impact on the Iraqi population, when it comes to active service, than on Iran's.

As for the composition of the Iraqi armed forces, it can be said that the biggest rate of increase has been in the army where numbers have increased from 190,000 in 1979/80 to 955,000 in 1987/8, followed by the air force which has increased its numbers from 28,000 to 40,000 in the same period.

Table 7.4 illustrates the list of major weapon systems held by the Iraqi forces for selected years since the war. At this point, it should

Table 7.4 Major weapon systems held by the armed forces: Iraq, 1979/80, 1980/1, 1984/5 and 1987/8

	1979/80	Change[a] %	1980/1	Change[a] %	1984/5[b]	Change[a] %	1987/8[b]
Tanks	1,900	50	2,850	73	4,920	28	6,310[c]
Combat aircraft	339	0	339	71	580	?	500+[d]
Helicopters	231	19	276	38	381	11	422
Armoured fighting vehicle	1,500	67	2,500	28	3,200	25	4,000

Notes: [a] Author's calculation.
[b] Due to losses and incomplete reporting of resupply, all figures tentative.
[c] Among them: some 4,500 T-54/55/-62/-72; 1,500 T-59/-69, 150 Chieftain, M-60, and M-47 (mostly captured from Iran).
[d] Among them: 1 squadron of TU-22, 1 squadron of TU-16, 4 squadrons of MIG-23BM, and 4 squadrons of Mirage F-IEQS (Exocet-equipped). As well as some 25 MIG-25; 40 MIG-19; 200 MIG-21 and 30 Mirage F-IEQ.
Sources: IISS 1979/80 to 1987/8

be emphasized that nowhere better can the difference in availability of military hardware to Iraq and Iran be observed than in tables 7.4 and 5.5. While, as noted before, Iran has been starved of any kind of weapons, table 7.4 shows that Iraq, on the other hand, has been suffering from a very serious case of obesity! In a nutshell, it must be said that the figures in table 7.4 are indeed 'unbelievable'.

As can be seen, the seven-year conflict, with all the destruction that it has caused in terms of weapons lost, none the less has resulted in the numbers of tanks, combat aircraft, helicopters and AFVs being increased by 232, 47, 83 and 167 per cent respectively, between 1979/80 and 1987/8.

In all, we must admit that the information provided in table 7.4 is mind-boggling to say the least. How can a country which has lost much of its oil revenues and all of its foreign reserves and has gone through a seven-year war end up with so much more military hardware than at the beginning of the war? In the following chapter an attempt is made to shed light on this issue.

Conclusion

In this chapter we have attempted to shed light on the militarization of Iraq since its invasion of Iran in 1980. It has been shown that, although since the war there has been a significant decline in Iraq's GDP (both including and excluding oil), there has also been a rapid increase in Milex, resulting in an unparalleled rise in the defence burden.

It was also noted that the value of arms imports has increased by 34 per cent on average each year during the 1980–5 period, representing an average defence burden of 27 per cent each year. By comparing the above figures with the pre-war period of 1973-9, we were able to demonstrate that indeed, since the war, there has been a massive increase.

It was also observed that, since the war, there has been a huge increase in the number of people under arms in Iraq. In fact, their number has increased by 350 per cent between 1979/80 and 1987/8. Thus the percentage share of the total population involved with the armed forces has increased from 1.7 to 17 per cent during the same period.

As for the quality and quantity of major weapon systems held by the Iraqi forces, we demonstrated that the numbers of tanks, combat aircraft, helicopters and AFVs too have increased by 232, 47, 83 and 167 per cent respectively since the war. In all, given the size of the Iraqi population, it can be argued that, since the war, Iraq has been turned into a 'military machine', with major consequences for the post-war period, as the readjustment to a more 'normal' life may prove too difficult.

Chapter eight

The Iran–Iraq war and the arms trade

Introduction

This is a chapter in which we hope to demonstrate the world's hypocrisy. We hope to establish beyond any reasonable doubt how immoral and indifferent the world has been in so far as the sales of arms to the areas of conflict, i.e. the Iran–Iraq war, are concerned.

Nowhere better in the world can one observe these low standards than in a study of arms sales to the warring countries in the Gulf. There is, it seems, hardly a country, in East or West, South or North, where the rules of the 'game' have not been allowed to be broken, so that weapons can be exported or re-exported to one or both countries.

Because of the extensive involvement of many countries, with numerous scandals and forging of documents, it is impossible to cover the entire subject in this chapter. Therefore, here, we will identify those countries that have supplied the necessary 'fuel' for the 'engine' of war and destruction in the Gulf. We will also demonstrate the connection between the duration of the war and the ever increasing number of suppliers of weapons to both countries.

Thus, at this stage, no attempt will be made to discuss the composition of the weapons delivered, or how the arms have been supplied, etc., although confirmed arms deliveries will be identified. However, the reader interested in following this subject further, is strongly encouraged to consult the works of Walter De Bock and Jean-Charles Deniau (1988), Anthony H. Cordesman (1987a), Michael Brzoska (1987), Thomas Ohlson and Elisabeth Skons (1987), Michael Brzoska and Thomas Ohlson (1986) and the Tower Commission Report (1987), amongst others.

Arms suppliers to Iran and Iraq since the war

Prior to the Iraqi invasion of Iran, there was already an embargo on arms sales to Iran, imposed by President Carter in reaction to the taking of American 'hostages' in Tehran.

Moreover, as noted in chapter two, the near disintegration of the regular armed forces in Iran soon after the revolution, as well as the departure of American military advisers, meant that Iran had major problems in operating its highly advanced weaponry systems at the time of the conflict.

Therefore, immediately after the invasion, the low level of operational ability of the armed forces and the newly created *Psadarans* had meant that Iran was in desperate need of unsophisticated and simply operated arms, including shells, bombs, dynamite, explosives, missiles, etc.

Moreover, Iran's need for such weapons coincided with the equally desperate need of many other countries to increase their conventional, unsophisticated arms sales. These sales had dropped significantly because of huge rises in the export of advanced weapons and military hardware following the oil-price increases of 1973–4.

Futhermore, as noted in previous chapters, the Soviet Union had reduced its arms exports to Iraq soon after its invasion of Iran. This had also created an opportunity for other countries to supply Iraq with much needed weapons.

The above factors, amongst others, had created a situation which may never have existed before. Namely, two very rich countries at war, both desperate for arms (Iran in particular), and both willing and able to pay huge sums for their supplies. Therefore the sky was the limit, so to speak, for the rest of the world to 'satisfy' them.

Tables 8.1a to 8.1c illustrate the extent of the world's involvement in supplying weapons to Iran and Iraq. Table 8.1a identifies the countries supplying arms and other support to Iran during the 1980–3 period. The corresponding information on Iraq is provided in table 8.1b. Table 8.1c lists the 'clever' countries, namely those who have been arming the two countries at the same time. These tables, in our view, can be taken as a starting point to show the hypocritical nature of the supplying nations.

By looking at these tables, it can be seen that by the end of 1983 there were 8 countries supplying arms to Iran only, while 9 countries were supplying Iraq. In the 'clever' category, there were 9 more countries supplying both Iran and Iraq. In all, during the same period, there were 26 suppliers of weapons to Iran and Iraq;

The economic consequences of the Gulf War

Table 8.1a Arms supply and other support to Iran, 1980–3

Countries supplying Iran only	Weapons[a]	Other support[b]	Major weapon supplier before the war
Greece	*	*	USA and Britain
Israel	*	*	
Syria	*	*	
Yemen, South		*	
Korea, South	*	*	
Taiwan		*	
Vietnam		*	
Algeria	*	*	
Libya	*	*	
South Africa	*		
Argentina	*	*	

Notes: [a] The term 'weapons' includes major weapons, small arms, ammunitions or explosives.
   [b] 'Other support' includes military transport vehicles, spare parts, training, military advisers, logistic support or financial support.
Source: Based on SIPRI 1984: 198, table 7.5

Table 8.1b Arms supply and other support to Iraq, 1980–3

Countries supplying Iraq only	Weapons[a]	Other support[b]	Major weapon supplier before the war
Belgium		*	Soviet Union and France
FR Germany	*	*	
Portugal		*	
Spain	*	*	
Czechoslovakia	*	*	
Hungary	*		
Poland	*	*	
Yugoslavia	*		
Austria	*		
Egypt	*	*	
Jordan	*	*	
Kuwait		*	
Saudi Arabia		*	
United Arab Emirates		*	
Pakistan		*	
Phillipines		*	
Morocco		*	
Ethiopia		*	
Sudan		*	

Notes: [a] The term 'weapons' includes major weapons, small arms, ammunitions or explosives.
   [b] 'Other support' includes military transport vehicles, spare parts, training, military advisers, logistic support or financial support.
Source: Based on SIPRI 1984: 198, table 7.5

Table 8.1c   Countries supplying arms to both Iran and Iraq, 1980–3

	Iran weapons[a]	Other support[b]	Iraq weapons[a]	Other support[b]
USA	*	*	*	
Soviet Union	*	*	*	*
China	*		*	
France	*	*	*	*
Italy	*	*	*	*
German DR	*		*	*
Switzerland	*		*	
Korea, North	*	*	*	*
Brazil	*	*	*	*

Notes: [a] The term 'weapons' includes major weapons, small arms, ammunitions or explosives.
   [b] 'Other support' includes military transport vehicles, spare parts, training, military advisers, logistic support or financial support.
Source: Based on SIPRI 1984: 198, table 7.5

'other' military-related support was also provided by some of the same countries as well as many more. (For more details see tables 8.1a to 8.1c)

Tables 8.2a to 8.2c illustrate the number of countries supplying arms or 'other' military-related support to Iran, Iraq or both, during the 1980–6 period. As shown in table 8.2a, by the end of 1986 there were 12 countries supplying weapons to Iran only. This

Table 8.2a   Arms supply and other supports to Iran, 1980–6

Supplying Iran only	Weapons[a]	Other support[b]
Algeria	*	*
Argentina	*	*
Canada	*	*
Denmark		*
Finland	*	
Israel	*	*
Kenya		*
Korea, South	*	*
Libya	*	*
Mexico	*	*
Singapore		*
Syria	*	*
Taiwan	*	*
Turkey	*	*
Vietnam	*	
Yemen, South		*

Notes: [a] The term 'weapons' includes major weapons, small arms, ammunitions or explosives.
   [b] 'Other support' includes military transport vehicles, spare parts, training, military advisers, logistic support or financial support.
Source: Based on SIPRI 1987: 204–5, table 7.8

Table 8.2b Arms supply and other supports to Iraq, 1980–6

Supplying Iraq only	Weapons[a]	Other support[b]
Egypt	*	*
Jordan	*	*
Kuwait		*
Morocco		*
Phillipines	*	*
Sudan		*
Tunisia		*
United Arab Emirates		*
Yemen, North		*

Notes: [a] The term 'weapons' includes major weapons, small arms, ammunitions or explosives.
   [b] 'Other support' includes military transport vehicles, spare parts, training, military advisers, logistic support of financial support.
Source: Based on SIPRI 1987: 204–5, table 7.8

Table 8.2c Countries supplying arms to both Iran and Iraq, 1980–6

Country supporting both parties	Iran weapons[a]	Other support[b]	Iraq weapons[a]	Other support[b]
Austria	*	*	*	
Belgium	*	*	*	
Brazil	*	*	*	*
Bulgaria	*	*	*	*
Chile	*		*	
China	*	*	*	*
Czechoslovakia	*	*	*	*
Ethiopia		*	*	
FR Germany	*	*	*	*
France	*		*	*
German DR	*	*	*	*
Greece	*	*	*	*
Hungary	*	*	*	*
Italy	*	*	*	*
Korea, North	*		*	
Netherlands	*		*	
Pakistan	*	*	*	*
Poland	*	*	*	*
Portugal	*		*	
Saudi Arabia		*	*	
South Africa	*		*	
Soviet Union	*	*	*	*
Spain	*		*	*
Sweden	*	*	*	
Switzerland	*		*	
UK	*	*	*	*
USA	*	*	*	*
Yugoslavia	*	*	*	*

Notes: [a] The term 'weapons' includes major weapons, small arms, ammunitions or explosives.
   [b] 'Other support' includes military transport vehicles, spare parts, training, military advisers, logistic support or financial support.
Source: Based on SIPRI 1987: 204–5, table 7.8

represents an increase of 4 countries since the 1980–3 period. The newcomers include Canada, Denmark, Finland and Singapore.

If we look at table 8.2b, it can be seen that there were only 3 countries, namely Egypt, Jordan and the Philippines, that were supplying Iraq only. This represents a decline of 6 countries since the 1980–3 period. A reason for this can be related to the huge increase in arms exports by the Soviet Union to Iraq since 1982/3 and thus to a lesser need for arms imports from other sources, supplying Soviet-made weapons. This can clearly be observed by noting that the countries that were *not* supplying Iraq only in the 1983–6 period, but *were* in 1980–3, included Czechoslovakia, Hungary, Poland and Yugoslavia.

The scale of the world's involvement in supplying arms to both Iran and Iraq can best be noted in table 8.2c. It can be seen that by 1986 there were 26 countries supplying weapons to both countries. This means that by the second period of the war (i.e. 1983 to 1986), 17 new countries had joined in arming both Iran and Iraq at the same time.

We noted that tables 8.1a to 8.1c were the start of the journey into hypocrisy. We have now reached our destination. Tables 8.2a to 8.2c are the final points of our journey. These tables represent the selfishness and lack of moral standards of 41 countries which have put their profits and self interest before their loyalty to fellow human beings elsewhere in the world.

One final thing that we would like to do is to draw the reader's attention to the fact that the Iran–Iraq war and the supply of arms to both countries are not the only examples of arms being delivered to an area of conflict.

In fact, the whole issue of arms sales to the Third World, where resources are scarce and the majority of governments are unable to provide for the basic needs of the population, must be brought to the forefront of world attention (i.e. the people of the major advanced economies). This is a vital issue, given the sums spent and, thus, the huge scale of opportunity cost incurred.[1]

For example, it has been estimated that during the 1982–6 period, the total value of arms exports from the leading major weapon exporting countries, namely the USA, the Soviet Union, France, the UK, FR Germany and Italy, has been the sum of $142,591 million at 1985 constant prices (SIPRI 1987: 183, table 7.1). A point to be noted is the fact that the greatest share of the global arms trade is not between the advance economies themselves, but with the Third World.

Indeed, during the same period, 51.6 per cent of total US arms exports were destined for the Third World. The corresponding figure for the Soviet Union is 76.1 per cent, France 86.1 per cent, the UK 66.5 per cent, FR Germany 62.9 per cent and Italy 98 per cent (SIPRI 1987: 183, table 7.1). The reader, at this point, is invited to compare and contrast the scale of arms sales to the countries of the Third World on the one hand, with their global indebtedness, hunger and poverty, to name but a few, on the other.

Given the scope and limit of this study, we cannot discuss this issue any further. However, it is hoped that, although very brief, we were able to highlight the scale of the militarization of the Third World, and the fact that the Iran–Iraq war is part and parcel of that militarization.

A further point to be noted is that the Iran–Iraq war has led to the rise of a few prominent Third World arms exporters, such as China and Brazil. As noted in *Business Week* (29 December 1986), these two countries have built up arms industries that are thriving as a result of the Iran–Iraq war. It has been estimated that Brazil's annual arms sales of $250 million at the time the war began had increased to $1.7 billion in 1986 (ibid.), with 37 per cent on average each year destined for Iraq during 1982 to 1986 (SIPRI 1987: 198, table 7.6). Given the direct and indirect Brazilian arms sales to Iran, it is estimated that the total share of Brazil's arms exports to the warring nations in the Gulf might be as high as 50 per cent.

China, thanks to the Gulf War, has also been able to increase its arms exports to the Third World. The total share of the developing countries' arms imports from China has increased from 1.7 per cent in 1977–81 to 4.3 per cent during 1982–6 (SIPRI 1987: 183, table 7.1). It is understood that the increased share is a result of arms sales to Iran and Iraq since the war. Indeed, during the 1982–6 period, the confirmed Chinese arms sales to the Third World (i.e. it does not include the re-export of Chinese weapons from other countries to Iran and Iraq) had amounted at 1985 constant prices to $4,902 million (SIPRI 1987: 183, table 7.1), representing 3.1 per cent of the world's total during the same period.

The Iran–Iraq war has also created a major boom in the re-export of arms in the Third World. The main arms re-exporters are Egypt, Jordan, Libya, North Korea and Syria. As noted before, all these countries deliver arms to one or other warring parties in the Gulf. Although it is very difficult to estimate the value of profits earned through re-export, it can be argued that the returns must have been substantial, to say the least.

Given the above, it seems that many countries in the Third World in one way or other, are thriving as a result of the war. An important question at this point is: what is the effect going to be on these countries now that the war has ended, and Iran and Iraq might return to more conventional arms imports and to their traditional suppliers? The effect on these countries, especially on Brazil and China which, as noted above, have developed a major arms industry as the result of the war, could be very serious indeed. As long as the war continued, there existed an easy and welcoming market for outside penetration. Therefore it can be argued that another consequence of the Gulf War is the unparalleled rise in the number of arms merchants in the Third World.

So far in our presentation, an attempt has been made to demonstrate the complexities of arms sales to Iran and Iraq, in terms of unconfirmed and 'unconventional' sales. However, at this point we are able to shed light on confirmed arms suppliers to both countries since the war. Tables 8.3–5 at the end of this chapter illustrate the arms agreements between Iraq and the Soviet Union, France and other major suppliers during the 1979–87 period. Table 8.6 provides the corresponding information for Iran.

These tables go a long way to establish the ability of Iraq to import much of its arms needs from its traditional suppliers on one hand, and the inability of Iran to obtain any large-scale replacements for most of its pre-war and US-supplied weapons on the other. At the same time, while Iraq has been able to receive more weapons, both in quality and quantity, in virtually every category, Iran has suffered badly in its inability to obtain high-performance and advanced weaponry systems.

In all, as can be seen, the Soviet Union and France, as in the pre-war period, have remained Iraq's major arms suppliers since the war, supplying the most modern and advanced arsenal of weapons. Brazil and Italy are other major suppliers to Iraq. Confirmed arms agreements with other countries include China, Egypt, Spain, Jordan, the UK and the USA. (For further details see table 8.5.)

In looking at table 8.6 it becomes clear that, in contrast to Iraq, there are not many confirmed arms agreements between Iran and other countries, hence the existence of, as noted before, a large 'grey' and 'black' market in arms exports to Iran.

Conclusion

This chapter was an illustration of the world's hypocrisy. We attempted to demonstrate how immoral and indifferent the world has been, in so far as the sales of arms to Iran and Iraq, i.e. countries at war, are concerned.

It was noted that there is hardly any country in East or West, South or North, where the rules of the 'game' have not been allowed to be broken, so that weapons can be exported or re-exported to one or both countries.

We observed that many factors, such as the US-imposed embargo on sales of arms to Iran, the low level of operational ability of the Iranian armed forces, the desire on the part of the suppliers to supply Iran with unsophisticated military hardware, and finally the actual reduction in the Soviet arms exports to Iraq soon after the invasion, had created a situation which had probably never existed before: namely, two very rich countries at war, desperate for arms and spare parts, and willing and able to pay large sums for their supplies.

In all, it was noted that, during the first part of the war (1980–3), there were 26 countries supplying all kinds of weapon to Iran and Iraq. This figure, however, had increased to 41 by the end of the second period (1983–6).

We also observed that the Gulf War has led to the rise of a few prominent Third World arms exporters, in particular China and Brazil, who have developed a thriving arms export business because of the Gulf War. We noted that, as long as the war continued, there existed an easy and welcoming market for outside penetration. However, this might not necessarily be the case now that the war has ended and Iran and Iraq might return to their more traditional arms suppliers. The consequences of such an action on Brazil and China could be profound, to say the least.

Table 8.3 Confirmed arms agreements between Iraq and the Soviet Union, 1979–87

Weapon designation	Weapon description	Year of order
11-18	Transport	1979
11-20	Transport	1979
11-76	Transport	1979
–	LST	1979
Scud-B	SSM	1979
–	Submarine	1979
T-72	MBT	1979
Mid-27	Fighter	1979
M-1973	SPH	1980
M-1974	SPH	1979
T-72	MBT	1980
SA-8 Geeko	SAM	1982
Mig-25	Fighter	1984
Mig-25	Fighter	1984
T-55	MBT	1984

Table 8.3 (continued)

Weapon designation	Weapon description	Year of order
T-62	MBT	1984
T-72	MBT	1984
AS-4 Kitchen	ASM	1983
AS-6 Kingfish	ALCM	1983
Mig-23 BN	Fighter	1984
SU-20	Fighter	1983
BTR-40PB	AAV(M)	1982
Mi-24	Hel	1986
Mig-23BN	Fighter	1986
Mig-29	Fighter	1986
BM-21	MRS	1986
BTR-80	APC	1986
M-1974	SPH	1986
T-74	MBT	1986

Note: For meaning of abbreviations, see pp. 155–7.
Sources: SIPRI 1979 to 1987

Table 8.4 Confirmed arms agreements between Iraq and France, 1979–87

Weapon designation	Weapon description	Year of order
ERC-90S Sagaie	AC	1979
HOT	ATM	1979
Mirage F-1C	Fighter	1979
R-440 Crotale	SAM	1979
SA-330L PUMA	Hel	1979
SA-342K	Hel	1979–80
Alpha Jet	Trainer	1981
Mirage F-1C	Fighter	1980
Roland-2	SAM	1981
Super Frelon	Hel	1981
AMX-30-155	SPG	1982
Mirage F-1C	Fighter	1982
Alpha Jet	Trainer/Fighter	1984
AM-39 Exocet	AShM	1983
Super Etendard	Fighter	1983
Mirage-5D	Fighter	1984
ARMAT	ARM	1984
AS-30L	ASM	1984
Alpha Jet	Trainer/Fighter	1986
Mirage F-1C	Fighter	1985
R-530	AAM	1985

Note: For meaning of abbreviations, see pp. 155–7.
Sources: SIPRI 1979 to 1987

Table 8.5 Confirmed arms agreements between Iraq and major arms suppliers (excluding the Soviet Union and France), 1979–87

Supplier	Weapon designation	Weapon description	Year of order
Brazil	EE-11	APC	1979
	EE-17	TD	1979
	EE-9	Recce AC	1979
	MAS-1	ASM	1980
	EE-3	SC	1982
	EE-11	APC	1982
	EE-11	APC	1983
	EE-9	AC	1984
	11-SS-30	MRS	1985
	EE-3	SC	1987
	EE-9	AC	1986
China	T-59	MBT	1981
	TYPE 531	APC	1982
	Type 69	MBT	1982
	T-69	MBT	1982
Egypt	AT-3	ATM	1981
	T-55	MBT	1981
	EMB-312	Trainer	1983
	F-6	Fighter	1983
	F-7	Fighter	1983
	T-55	MBT	1983
Italy	AB-212	Hel	1980
	SH-3D	Hel	1980
	–	ShAM/ShShM	1979
	–	ShShM	1979
	–	Submarine	1980
	–	Tanker	1979
	–	Corvette	1979
	–	Frigate	1979
	A-109	Hel	1984
	AB-212	Hel	1984
Indonesia	BO-105CB	Hel	1980
Switzerland	PC-7	Trainer	1981
German DR	T-54/T-55	MBT	1980
German FR	BO-105CB	Hel	1984
	BK-117	Hel	1984
Poland	T-55	MBT	1980
	SA-6	SAM	1985
Yugoslavia	T-72	MBT	1980
	–	Frigate	1979
Spain	BMR-600	ICV	1981
	C-101	Trainer	1981
	C-212-200	Transport	1981
	BO-105CB	Hel	1980
Jordan	Khalid	MBT	1982
	GHN-45	TH/TG	1982
	F-6	Fighter	1983
	GHN-45	TH/TG	1984

Table 8.5 (continued)

Supplier	Weapon designation	Weapon description	Year of order
Saudi Arabia	FG-70	TH	1986
Kuwait	Chieftain-5	MBT	1984
UK	Sabateur	APC	1982
USA	L-100-30	Transport	1982
	214ST	Hel	1985

Note: For meaning of abbreviations, see pp. 155–7.
Source: SIPRI 1984: table 7.5

Table 8.6 Confirmed arms agreements between Iran and major arms suppliers, 1979–87

Supplier	Weapon designation	Weapon description	Year of order
Libya	T-54	MBT	1981
	T-55	MBT	1981
	T-66	MBT	1981
	SCUD-B	SAM	1986
Syria	T-55	MBT	1982
	T-62	MBT	1982
	SCUD-B	SSM	1984
Argentina	TAM	Tank	1983
China	F-6	Fighter	1983
	T-59	MBT	1985
	130 mm	TG	1985
	122 mm	TG	1985
	CSA-1	SAM	1985
	HY-5	SAM	1985
	F-7	Fighter	1985
	CSA-1 Sams	SAM System	1985
North Korea	T-62	Tank	1981
	F-6	Fighter	1985
	SA-2	SAM	1985
South Korea	–	LS	1984
UK	–	LS	1977 (delivered since the war)
	KhaBg type	Support ship	1974 (delivered since the war)
	AR-3D	3-D radar	1986
	Watchman	Radar	1987
USA	AIM-9L	AAM	1985 (150 delivered)
	MIM-23B Hawk	SAM	1986 (235 delivered)
	BGM-71A Tow	ATM	1986 (2,008 delivered)
Vietnam	F-5E	Fighter	1986
	UH-H	Hel	1986
	M-107	SPG	1986
	M-113-A1	APC	1986
	M-48	MBT	1986
	AIM-9E	AAM	1986

Note: For meaning of abbreviations, see pp. 155–7.
Source: Based on SIPRI 1987

Chapter nine

The impact of the war on the military expenditure and arms imports of Saudi Arabia and Kuwait

Introduction

The revolution in Iran, the rise of Shi'ite fundamentalism in largely Sunni-Muslim-dominated countries in the Persian Gulf and the Soviet invasion of Afghanistan were among the main reasons for a rapid increase in military expenditure and arms imports in the Gulf countries in the late 1970s.

However, the present security threats, arising from the Gulf War, have resulted in a more rapid militarization and further acquisition of weapons in the neighbouring countries. Since 1979/80 all the six Gulf Co-operation Council (GCC) members have spent billions of dollars on importing major sophisticated weapon systems. It is important to note that such rapid increases in military expenditure (Milex) and arms imports have taken place at a time when oil revenues have been falling, and therefore resources have become more scarce. This obviously has a profound economic effect on the economies of these countries. Futhermore, given the small size of the population in these countries, the wisdom of receiving such advanced weapons in such quantities can seriously be questioned.

This chapter is divided into two parts. The first provides a brief study of Milex in and arms imports by Saudi Arabia and Kuwait. It is expected that this presentation will more clearly establish the case that the Gulf has been further militarized since the war. The second attempts to assess the cost of high military burdens arising from militarization in the cases of Saudi Arabia and Kuwait, especially in terms of forgoing potential foreign exchange.

Milex and arms imports, Saudi Arabia and Kuwait: 1973–85

Table 9.1 provides information on the value of Milex and the ratio of defence burden of Saudi Arabia and Kuwait during the 1973–85

Table 9.1 Ratio of military expenditures (Milex) in GDP – defence burden*, Kuwait and Saudi Arabia, 1973–85

	GDP Kuwait BN. (K) dinars	Kuwait's Milex BN. (K) dinars	Kuwait's defence burden*	GDP (Saudi BN. (S) rials)	Saudi's Milex BN. (S) rials	Saudi's defence burden
1973	2.2	0.074	3.4	40.6	4.3	10.6
1974	3.5	0.179	5.1	99.3	9.2	9.3
1975	3.2	0.210	6.6	139.6	23.7	17.0
1976	3.8	0.312	8.2	164.5	32.4	19.7
1977	3.9	0.300	7.7	205.1	32.7	15.9
1978	4.2	0.309	7.4	223.8	35.9	16.1
1979	6.7	0.339	5.1	248.4	46.7	18.8
1980	7.8	0.400	5.1	385.8	57.2	14.8
1981	6.9	0.478	6.9	520.6	83.0	15.9
1982	6.1	0.476	7.8	524.7	92.1	17.6
1983	6.3	0.429	6.8	415.2	95.2	22.9
1984	6.6	0.491	7.4	371.3	79.4	21.4
1985	5.9	0.548	9.3	339.2	64.0	18.9

Average annual growth of GDP* 1973–8   Kuwait 13.8% Saudi 40.7%
Average annual growth of GDP 1979–85   Kuwait −2.1% Saudi 5.3%
Average annual growth of Milex* 1973–8   Kuwait 33.1% Saudi 52.9%
Average annual growth of Milex* 1979–85   Kuwait 8.3%   Saudi 5.4%

Average annual defence burden* 1973–8
Kuwait   Saudi
6.4%   14.8%

Average annual defence burden* 1979–85
Kuwait   Saudi
6.9%   18.6%

Note: * Author's calculation. All the figures quoted are in local currency and at current prices.
Sources: IMFa 1980/2 and 1986; OPEC 1985; and IISS 1973/4 to 1986/7

period. As can be seen, in 1973 and 1974 (before OPEC I), Saudi Arabia had spent 4.3 billion riyals and 9.2 billion riyals on Milex. Then, as a result of the oil-price increases, Milex had increased to 23.7 billion riyals in 1975, representing an increase of 167 per cent. Since 1976 and up to 1978 (i.e. the start of the Iranian revolution), the Saudis' Milex had remained at between 32–36 billion riyals.

However, since the revolution and the Iraqi invasion of Iran, the Saudis' Milex has been increased at an amazingly high rate. By 1980, Milex had increased to 57.2 billion riyals, representing an increase of 58 per cent since 1978. The corresponding figures for 1983 were 95.2 billion riyals and 164 per cent.

As a result of the rapid decrease in oil prices in recent years, Milex has correspondingly fallen to 64 billion riyals in 1985. In all, during the 1978–83 period, Milex had increased by 21 per cent on average each year, while GDP had grown by 13 per cent. The corresponding figures for the 1978–85 period, to take account of the decline in oil prices, were 9 and 6 per cent on average each year.

As far as Milex in Kuwait is concerned, it can be seen that again as a result of oil-price increases in 1973/4, Milex had increased, by 1975, to 0.210 billion dinars, representing an increase of 184 per cent since 1973. However, since the initial increase in Milex, the expenditure had remained at about 0.300 billion dinars up to 1978.

Since 1978 Milex and defence burdens have rapidly increased. Milex has grown by an average annual rate of 8.5 per cent during the 1978–85 period, while the corresponding figure for GDP growth is only 4.9 per cent (see further table 9.1). Moreover, by 1985 the defence burden had increased significantly to 9.3 per cent from 5.1 per cent in 1981.

Table 9.2 provides information on the estimated value of arms imports as well as the burden of arms imports in Saudi Arabia and Kuwait during the 1973–85 period. It can be seen that, in Saudi Arabia, the value of estimated arms imports increased from 2.2 billion riyals in 1973 to 16.4 billion riyals in 1977, representing an increase of over 65 per cent on average each year during this period. However, as a result of security threats (real or imagined) since the late 1970s, there has been a massive rise in the estimated value of arms imports.

In fact, by 1983, the estimated value of arms imports had increased to 57.1 billion riyals, representing an increase of 23 per cent on average each year since 1977. As for the arms-imports burden, it can be noted that, while in 1978 there was a 21 per cent burden, by 1985 it had increased to 29.5 per cent. (For more details see table 9.2.)

Table 9.2 The ratio of arms imports in total imports – burden of arms imports[a], Saudi Arabia and Kuwait, 1973–85

	Saudi Arabia			Kuwait		
	Estimated arms imports[b] A	Non-military imports B	$\frac{A}{A+B}$ %	Estimated arms imports A	Non-military imports[b] B	$\frac{A}{A+B}$ %
1973	2.2	7.3	23.2	0.04	0.271	12.9
1974	4.6	10.2	30.1	0.09	0.456	16.5
1975	11.9	14.8	44.6	0.11	0.632	17.4
1976	16.2	30.7	34.5	0.16	1.0	13.8
1977	16.4	51.7	24.1	0.15	1.2	11.1
1978	17.9	69.2	21.0	0.16	1.3	10.9
1979	28.0	82.2	25.5	0.20	1.5	11.8
1980	34.3	96.2	26.0	0.24	1.7	12.4
1981	49.8	120.0	29.0	0.29	2.1	12.1
1982	55.3	138.2	28.4	0.29	2.3	11.2
1983	57.1	137.1	29.4	0.26	2.2	10.6
1984	47.6	118.0	29.0	0.29	2.2	12.7
1985	38.4	90.2	29.5	0.33	1.7	16.3
Total in bn. US$	110.3	272	–	8.7	61.2	–

Notes: [a] Authors' calculation. All the figures, except those in the last row, are in current local currency, billion riyals for Saudi Arabia and billion dinars for Kuwait.

[b] Military-related imports have been estimated at 50 and 60 per cent of the total military expenditure for each year during the 1973–8 and 1979–85 periods respectively. These assumptions are based on the actual value and volume of arms transfers to these countries. We, however, admit that these are at best only educated guesses.

Sources: IMFa 1980 and 1986; IMFb 1980 and 1987; IISS 1973/4 to 1986/7; SIPRI 1974 to 1987; and USACDA 1969–78 and 1985

In Kuwait also there has been a rapid rise in the estimated value of arms imports. Indeed they have increased from 0.16 billion dinars in 1978 to 0.33 billion dinars in 1985, representing an average annual increase of 11 per cent during the same period. The arms-imports-burden ratio has correspondingly increased from 10.9 to 16.3 per cent during the same period.

In all, table 9.2 demonstrates very clearly and beyond an/doubt how these two countries, in particular Saudi Arabia, witn small populations, in absolute, as well as relative terms, have become a storage place for the weapon makers of the industrialized countries.

It can be seen from the list of confirmed arms suppliers to Saudi Arabia and Kuwait during the 1973–8 period, which is illustrated in tables 9.7 and 9.8 at the end of this chapter, that, during this period, the USA was the major supplier of weapons to Saudi Arabia, followed by France and the UK. Many different types of weapons, including fighters, tanks, helicopters, armoured personnel carriers and many different sorts of missiles, have been supplied by these countries.

Arms acquisitions by the Kuwaitis are much smaller in value and quantity. Major suppliers include the USA, France and the UK. The Soviets had also joined in providing weapons to Kuwait, among them SAM missiles.

Tables 9.9–11 illustrate the list of arms suppliers to Saudi Arabia during the 1979–87 period. From these tables it becomes clear that the USA is by far the major supplier of arms to Saudi Arabia, followed by France and the UK. To arrive at an accurate share of each supplier, in the Saudis' total arms imports, given the availability of information at present, is apparently an impossible task. However, having analysed the tables, and noted the quantity and quality of arms supplied, we estimate that the USA has had a 55 per cent share of the Saudis' arms imports, followed by France and the UK (jointly) 40 per cent, and the 'others' 5 per cent. We, however, admit that these are 'educated' guesses only.

Therefore, given our estimates, the value of arms exports by the USA to Saudi Arabia during the 1973–85 period is the total of $60.6 billion. The corresponding figure for France and the UK (jointly) is $44.1 billion.

These three countries, between them have supplied such an arsenal of weapons to Saudi Arabia that, one wonders, given the small size of the population, by whom or how these weapons are going to be used if, or when, there is a military need for their use. The seriousness of this problem will be seen at a later date when the Iran–Iraq war has ended. The security threat would therefore be removed, and the Saudis could find it too difficult to produce any justification for maintaining such a high military portfolio.

In all, as shown in tables 9.9 and 9.10, every kind of weapon possible, especially of the most advanced types, has been delivered to Saudi Arabia. The militarization of Saudi Arabia at such a break-neck speed will have a major impact on the post-war development of countries like Iran. Is Iran, in the post-war period, going to accept a lesser militarized posture than a country like Saudi Arabia, or is it going for a rapid build-up of its armed forces, accompanied by a massive increase in arms imports? If the second option is adopted, then there will be serious competition, given scarce resources, for the development of the civilian economy.

Table 9.12 illustrates the list of countries supplying arms to Kuwait. It can be seen that, in this case also, the USA, France and the UK are the main beneficiaries of increased arms imports by the Kuwaitis. They have, among themselves, provided the most advanced weapon system to a country of only 1.8 million people. How and under what conditions these weapons can be used by the Kuwaiti citizens remains to be seen.

Table 9.3 provides information on the quantity and composition of major weapon systems held by the Saudi and Kuwaiti armed forces during the 1972/3 to 1987/8 period. It can be seen that the number of tanks in Saudi Arabia has increased from 85 to 550 during the same period. The corresponding figures for combat aircraft, helicopters and AFVs were 71, 30 and 200, rising to 226, 91 and 550 during the same period.

Table 9.3 Major weapon systems held by the armed forces, Saudi Arabia and Kuwait, 1972/3, 1979/80, 1984/5, 1986/7 and 1987/8

		1972/3[a]	*1979/80*	*1984/5*	*1986/7*	*1987/8*
Tanks	(S)	85	350	450	450	550
	(K)	100	280[b]	240[b]	230[b]	160[b]
Combat aircraft	(S)	71	178	203	216	226
	(K)	28	50	49	80	80
Helicopters	(S)	30	52	60	80	91
	(K)	7	44	35	40	40
Armoured fighting vehicle	(S)	200	200	200	550	550
	(K)	?	120	160	160	160

Notes: (S) Saudi Arabia.
    (K) Kuwait.
    ? Not known exactly.
    [a] For Kuwait (1974/5).
    [b] The numbers of tanks in Kuwait falling since 1979/80 may be because most of them have been given to the Iraq army.
Sources: IISS 1972/3 to 1987/8

As for Kuwait, it can be noted that the number of tanks had increased from 100 in 1972/3 to 280 in 1979/80. However, this figure has declined to 160 in 1987/8. Therefore it is most likely that Kuwait, besides any other assistance it has provided to Iraq, has also supplied that country with many tanks. The number of combat aircrafts and helicopters on the other hand has increased from 28 and 7 to 80 and 40 during the same period.

Table 9.4 provides information on military manpower and its composition in Saudi Arabia and Kuwait during the period under study. As can be noted, in Saudi Arabia, between 1972/3 and 1979/80, the total military manpower had increased from 41,000 to 45,000, representing an average annual growth rate of 1.3 per cent.

Table 9.4 Military manpower and its composition, Saudi Arabia and Kuwait, 1972/3, 1979/80, 1980/1, 1984/5, 1986/7 and 1987/8 (thousands)

		1972/3[a]	*1979/80*	*1980/1*	*1984/5*	*1986/7*	*1987/8*
Total	(S)	41.0	45.0	48.0[b]	52.0[c]	48.0[c]	67.0[c]
	(K)	10.2	11.2	12.5[d]	12.5[d]	13.1[d]	16.1[d]
of which:							
Army	(S)	36.0	35.0	31.0	35.0	40.0	45.0
	(K)	8.0	9.0	10.0	10.0	10.0	13.0
Air force	(S)	4.0	8.0	15.0	14.0	14.0	15.0
	(K)	2.0	2.0	2.0	2.0	2.0	2.0
Navy	(S)	1.0	2.0	2.0	3.0	4.0	4.0
	(K)	0.2	0.2	0.5	0.5	1.1	1.1

Notes: (S) Saudi Arabia.
(K) Kuwait.
[a] For Kuwait (1974/5).
[b] Up to the end of 1979, military service in Saudi Arabia was voluntary; in 1980 conscription was introduced.
[c] Does not include foreign contract military personnel, estimated at 10,000 in 1987/8.
[d] Excluding expatriate personnel.
The figures above do not include paramilitary forces.
Sources: IISS 1972/3 to 1987/8

However, in 1980, conscription was introduced. Therefore, the figures for military manpower have increased to 67,000 in 1987/8, representing an average annual growth rate of 5.1 per cent since 1979. It is also important to note that this figure does not include foreign contract military personnel, estimated at about 10,000 in 1987/8.

The number of military personnel in Kuwait has also increased significantly. Their numbers increased from 10,200 in 1974/5 to 11,200 in 1979/80, representing an average annual growth rate of 1.9 per cent.

Since 1980, however, the total military manpower has increased to 16,100, which represents an average growth rate of 5 per cent per year since 1979.

Once again, these two tables go a long way to demonstrate the rate at which Saudi Arabia and Kuwait have so rapidly been militarized since the Iran–Iraq war.

The opportunity cost of the militarization of Saudi Arabia and Kuwait: 1973–85

At this point an attempt is made to assess the cost of high military burdens arising from militarization, in terms of potential foreign-exchange reserves forgone for Saudi Arabia and Kuwait.

In a choice situation the concept of opportunity costs refers to the benefits forgone by selecting one option at the expense of several others. When resources are scarce, if a society (i.e. the government) selects policy A, it forgoes the benefits derived from policies B and C. The classic illustration of opportunity costs for governmental decision-making is the 'guns vs. butter' dilemma. This dilemma depicts spending on the military and social welfare as inversely related to one another. As Milex rises, the benefits of alternative preferences in the areas of social welfare must suffer.[1]

However, it seems, given the massive oil revenues, especially since the early 1970s, the oil-exporting countries in the Gulf have not, in a real sense, faced a 'guns vs. butter' dilemma, in so far as social welfare expenditure is concerned. Therefore it can be argued that, given the serious problem of absorptive-capacity constraints that has been persistent in these countries, the most serious opportunity cost of the rapid increases in Milex in the Persian Gulf countries is the potential losses in their foreign-exchange reserves.

Therefore here the focus is to try to estimate the dollar value of the potential foreign-exchange reserves that could have been possible, if a lesser share of the GDP had been allocated to Milex. The purpose of this endeavour is not to shed light on past losses, but to identify the areas in which future gains can be made.

In 1979, after the revolution, as noted in preceding chapters, the revolutionary government in Iran reduced the country's defence burden to a 4.5 per cent share of the GDP. This 'action' could have been followed by a 'reaction' from other countries in the region.[2] If it had, then less would have been spent on Milex. Therefore what we intend to do is to estimate what Saudi Arabia and Kuwait could have accumulated in foreign-exchange reserves, if they had followed Iran's example and had reduced their Milex to a level of a

Table 9.5 The opportunity cost of Saudi Arabia's military expenditures (Milex) in terms of foreign-exchange reserves forgone,* through inability to keep Milex at 4.5 per cent of GDP each year, 1973–85

	Actual GDP	Actual Milex A	Actual share of Milex in GDP %	Milex should have been, given our assumptions (4.5% of GDP/ year) B	Sums could have been available for investment abroad, given our assumptions [A–B]	US certificate-of-deposit rate %	Foreign-exchange reserves, including interests earned (compounded)	Equivalent in bn. US $
1973	40.6	4.3	10.6	1.8	2.5	6.95	–	–
1974	99.3	9.2	9.3	4.5	4.7	7.82	2.67	0.76
1975	139.6	23.7	17.0	6.3	17.4	7.49	7.98	2.28
1976	164.5	32.4	19.7	7.4	25.0	6.77	27.3	7.81
1977	205.1	32.7	15.9	9.2	23.5	6.69	55.84	15.95
1978	223.8	35.9	16.1	10.1	25.8	8.29	84.61	24.88
1979	248.4	46.7	18.8	11.2	35.5	11.22	119.55	35.16
1980	385.8	57.2	14.8	17.4	39.8	13.07	172.5	53.91
1981	520.5	83.0	15.9	23.4	59.6	15.91	240.04	70.60
1982	524.7	92.1	17.6	23.7	68.4	12.35	347.27	102.14
1983	415.2	95.2	22.9	18.7	76.5	9.09	467.03	133.44
1984	371.3	79.4	21.4	16.7	62.7	10.37	592.91	169.40
1985	339.2	64.0	18.9	15.3	48.7	8.05	723.59	206.77
1986							834.47	231.79

Notes: * Author's calculation. The figures quoted are all in bn. Saudi Arabian riyals, except where otherwise indicated.
Sources: IMFa 1980; 1982 and 1986; OPEC 1985 and IISS 1973/4–1986/7

Table 9.6 The opportunity cost of Kuwait's military expenditures (Milex) in terms of foreign-exchange reserves forgone,* through inability to keep Milex at 4.5 per cent of GDP each year, 1973–85

	Actual GDP	Actual Milex	Actual share of Milex in GDP	Milex should have been, given our assumptions (4.5% of GDP/ year)	Sums should have been available for investment abroad, given our assumptions	US certificate-of-deposit rate	Foreign-exchange reserves, including interests earned (compounded)	Equivalent in bn. US $
		A	%	B	[A–B]	%		
1973	2.2	0.074	3.4	–	–	–	–	–
1974	3.5	0.179	5.1	0.157	0.022	7.82	–	–
1975	3.2	0.210	6.6	0.144	0.066	7.49	0.024	0.08
1976	3.8	0.312	8.2	0.171	0.141	6.77	0.096	0.32
1977	3.9	0.300	7.7	0.176	0.124	6.69	0.253	0.84
1978	4.2	0.309	7.4	0.189	0.120	8.29	0.402	1.34
1979	6.7	0.339	5.1	0.302	0.037	11.22	0.562	1.87
1980	7.8	0.400	5.1	0.351	0.049	13.07	0.669	2.23
1981	6.9	0.478	6.9	0.311	0.167	15.91	0.813	2.71
1982	6.1	0.476	7.8	0.275	0.201	12.35	1.135	3.78
1983	6.3	0.429	6.8	0.284	0.145	9.09	1.501	5.00
1984	6.6	0.491	7.4	0.297	0.194	10.37	1.796	5.99
1985	5.9	0.548	9.3	0.266	0.282	8.05	2.195	7.32
1986							2.676	8.92

Notes: * Author's calculation. All figures quoted are in billion current Kuwaiti dinars, except those where otherwise indicated.
Sources: IMFa 1980, 1982 and 1986; OPEC 1985; and IISS 1973/4 to 1986/7.

4.5 per cent defence burden. (We assume implicitly that this share corresponds to the utility of the nations concerned.) A corresponding estimate for Iran and Iraq will be provided in the following chapter.

Furthermore, in order to expand the period under study and to highlight the scale of the opportunity costs in terms of foreign-exchange reserves forgone, we have extended the period under observation to cover the 1973–85 period. This is in order to find out what the above countries could have accumulated in foreign-exchange reserves, if at the very early stages of the oil-price increases they had agreed on a 4.5 per cent defence burden across the board.

Tables 9.5 and 9.6 illustrate the opportunity cost of Saudi Arabia and Kuwait's Milex in terms of foreign-exchange reserves forgone by not maintaining a 4.5 per cent defence burden each year during the 1973–85 period.

It can be seen that, if these countries had spent only 4.5 per cent of their annual GDP on Milex each year (in itself, a very large sum, given the large size of their GDPs in absolute and relative terms), they could have accumulated a significant sum in their foreign-exchange reserves.

The opportunity cost is much more profound in the case of Saudi Arabia which has spent a very large share of its GDP on defence (see table 9.5).

In all, if a 4.5 per cent defence burden had been maintained in Saudi Arabia and the difference between the actual and potential Milex (given our assumption) had been invested abroad, then, by the end of 1986, its compounded value could have increased to $231.8 billion. The corresponding figure for Kuwait is $8.9 billion.

Conclusion

This chapter was an attempt to demonstrate the impact of the revolution in Iran, the consequent rise of Shi'ite fundamentalism in the Gulf and the Iran–Iraq war on the pattern of Milex and arms imports in Saudi Arabia and Kuwait.

It was noted that in Saudi Arabia, the Milex has increased by 9 per cent on average each year during the 1978–85 period. The corresponding figure for Kuwait is 8.5 per cent. It was also estimated that a major part of such expenditure has been on imports of major sophisticated weapon systems, mainly from the USA, France and the UK. Indeed, given our assumption, it was noted that, during the 1973–85 period, the Saudis' arms imports had amounted to $110.3 billion. The corresponding figure for

Kuwait is $8.7 billion. It was observed that the USA has accounted for 55 per cent of such imports, followed by the UK and France 40 per cent and 'others' 5 per cent.

It was also noted that, since the war, military manpower in Saudi Arabia and Kuwait has been significantly increased. In fact, their numbers in both countries have increased by 5 per cent on average each year during the 1979–85 period. The corresponding figure for each country during the pre-war period was below 2 per cent on average each year.

Therefore it can be argued that another major consequence of the Iran–Iraq war has been the rapid militarization of the neighbouring countries in terms of increases in their Milex, arms imports and the number of military personnel.

This chapter also noted that, if both Saudi Arabia and Kuwait had maintained a 4.5 per cent defence burden each year during the 1973–85 period, they could have increased their potential foreign-exchange reserves significantly.

We noted that, if the difference between the actual and potential Milex (given our assumption) had been invested abroad, then, by the end of 1986, the Saudis' could have increased their potential foreign reserves by nearly $232.0 billion. The corresponding figure for Kuwait was estimated at nearly $9.0 billion.

As noted above, the purpose in estimating the potential losses resulting from a high military burden has not been to shed tears on past losses, but to identify the areas in which future gains can be made.

It is hoped that, given the result of our estimates, the significance of the potential foreign-exchange reserves forgone, will encourage further research into this subject for these countries, an area that, to the best of our knowledge, has not received enough or, for that matter, any attention at all.

Table 9.7 Confirmed arms suppliers to Saudi Arabia, 1973–8

Supplier	Weapon designation	Weapon description	Year of order
USA	Raytheon Hawk	S-A missile	1973
UK	Sea King (for Egypt)	Helicopter	1973
France	Commando (for Egypt)	Helicopter	1973
	Dassault Mirage 11E	Fighter	1973
	Dassault Mirage 111D	Trainer	1973
	Aerospatiale Aloutte 111	Helicopter	1974
	Dassault Mirage 111E	Fighter	1974
	Dassault Mirage 5 (for Egypt)	Fighter	1973
	Aerospatiale SS.11	A-T missile	1974
	Chatium	S-A missile	1974

Table 9.7 (continued)

Supplier	Weapon designation	Weapon description	Year of order
	AMX-30	Tank	1974
	AMX 101	Tank	1974
Pakistan	Warship	–	1974
USA	Bell AH-1J	Helicopter	1974
	Lockheed C-130 Hercules	Transport	1974
	Lockheed KC-130H	Tanker-Transport	1974
	Northrop F-5E Tiger 11	Fighter	1973
	Northrop F-5E Tiger 11	Fighter	1975
	Hughes Maverick	A-S missile	1975
	Hughes Maverick	A-T missile	1975
	MIM-23B	S-A missile	1974
	Armoured personnel carrier	–	1975
	M-60A1	Tank	1975
	Destroyer and guided missile	–	1974
	Lockheed C-130 Hercules	Transport	1975
	Northrop F-5E/F	Fighter	1975
	Hughes Maverik	ASM	1975
	McDonnell-Douglas Harpoon	ShShM	1975
FR Germany	Rheinstahl Marder	APC	1976
France	Dassault Mirage F-1	Fighter	1976
	Aerospatiale Harpoon	ATM	1974
	Aerospatiale/MBB Roland	ATM	1974
	Crotale	ShShM	1976
	Matra R.550 Magic	AAM	1973, 1975
	AMX-10	Armoured Car	1976
	Aerospatiale Alouette 111	Helicopter	1975
	Dassault Mirage F1	Fighter	1975
	AMX-30SA	SPA/A gun	1974
France/ FR Germany	Euromissile Roland	ATM	1974
UK	BAC 167 Mk 81	Trainer	1976
	BAC Rapier	SAM	1975
	Fox	Scout Car	1974
	Alvis Scorpion	Tank	1974
	Bell AH-1 Cobra	Helicopter	1975
	Morthrop F-5E	Fighter	1976
	G.E. Vulcan	AIA Gun	1976
	Hughes BGM-71 Tow	ATM	1976
	FGM-77A	ATM	1976
	AIM-9J-1 Sidewinder	AAM	1976
	322″-Class	Minesweeper	1975
	AIM-9J Sidewinder	AAM	1975
	F-5E Tiger-2	Trainer	1976
Italy	S-61A-4	Helicopter	1977
France	AML-90	AC	1976
	AMX-30s	MBT	1977
	MM-40 Exocet	ShShM	1976

Table 9.7 (continued)

Supplier	Weapon designation	Weapon description	Year of order
	P-32	PB	1976
USA	Bell-209-AH-1S	Helicopter	1978
	Bell-212	Helicopter	1978
	Boeing 747-131	Transport	1976
	C130H Hercules	Transport	1976
	F-15A Eagle	Fighter	1978
	TF-15A Eagle	Trainer	1978
	M-113-A1	ICV	1978
	M-60-A1	MBT	1976
	V-150	APC	1977
	AIM-7F Sparrow	AAM	1978
	AIM-9J	AAM	1978
	MIM-23B Hawk	SAM	1975
	MIM-43A Redeye	SAM	1976
	–	FPB	
	MSC-322	Minesweeper	
	–	CPB	
	–	Corvette	

Note: For meanings of abbreviations, see pp. 155–7.
Source: SIPRI 1972–3 to 1979

Table 9.8 Confirmed arms suppliers to Kuwait 1973–8

Supplier	Weapon designation	Weapon description	Year of order
France	Aerospatiale SA-330 Puma	Helicopter	1974
	Aerospatiale SA-341 Gazelle	Helicopter	1974
	Dassault Mirage F-1 (for Egypt)	Fighter	1974
	SS-11	ATM	1974
	Harpoon	ATM	1974
	HOT	ATM	1974
	Matria Magic (for Egypt)	AAM	1973
Singapore	Patrol boat	Displ: 25T	1973
USA	A-4 Skyhawk	Bomber	1974
	Hawk	SAM	1974
UK	Centurian	MBT	1976
Singapore	Vosper Thornycroft	Landing Ship	1974
France	Dassault Mirage F-1/C/B	Fighter	1973
	Matria 530/550 Magic	AAM	1973
UK	Chieftain	Tank	1976
USA	DC-9	Transport	1975
	BGN-71-TOW	ATM	1973
	MIM-23B	SAM	1974
	AIM-23B	AAM	1975
	M-113-A1	APC	1976
	A-4M Skyhawk	Bomber	1975
	C-9B Skytrain 11	Transport	1976
	TA-4K Skyhawk	Trainer	1975

Table 9.8 (continued)

Supplier	Weapon designation	Weapon description	Year of order
USSR	SA-7	SAM portable	1977
France	Crotale	SAM	
	Mirage F-1C	Fighter	1973
	MM-38 Exocet	ShShM	1977
	R-550 Magic	AAM intercept	1973
UK	Chieftain Mk5	MBT	1977
	BAC	TSA	1977
	Vosper	MAFB	1977
	BAC	Fighter	1977
	Vosper	FIB	1977
USSR	SA-6 Gainful	SAM	1978
	SA-7 Grail	Landmob/Post	1978
Singapore	–	LC	1977

Note: For meanings of abbreviations, see pp. 155–7.
Source: SIPRI 1972–3 to 1979

Table 9.9 Confirmed arms agreements between Saudi Arabia and the USA, 1979–87

Weapon designation	Weapon description	Year of order
AGM-65A	ASM	1979
AIM-9P	AAM	1979
FGM-77A	ATM	1979
M-113-A1	ICV	1979
M-577-A1	Cargo	1979
M-60-A1	MBT	1979
M-88-A1	ARV	1979
RGM-84A	ShShM	1979
C-130H	Transport	1979
E-3A	AEW	1980
F-15c	Fighter	1980
KC-130h	Transport	1979
M-110-A1	SPH	1980
V-150	APC	1979
AIM-9P	AAM	1980
TOW	ATM	1980
AIM-9L	AAM	1981
TOW	ATM	1982
F-5E	Fighter	1982
F-5F	Trainer	1982
M-198	TH	1981
RF-5E	Recce	1982
AGM-65D	ASM	1984
TOW	ATM	1983
N-1	MBT	1983
N-109-A2	SPH	1983
M-113-A2	APC	1983
N-198	TH	1983

Table 9.9 (continued)

Weapon designation	Weapon description	Year of order
M-60-A3	MBT	1983
KC-10A	Tanker	1984
AIM-9L	AAM	1984
FIM-92A	SAM	1984
Gulfstream 3	Transport	1983
UH-60 Blackhawk	Hel	1986
M-88-A1	ARV	1985
AN-TPS-32	3D-Radar	1985
AN-TPS-43	3D-Radar	1985
AGM-65D	ASM	1984
AGM-84A	AshM	1986
AIM-9L	AAM	1986
AIM-9P	AAM	1986

Note: For meanings of abbreviations, see pp. 155–7.
Source: SIPRI 1979 to 1987

Table 9.10 Confirmed arms agreements between Saudi Arabia and France/UK, 1979–87

Supplier	Weapon designation	Weapon description	Year of order
France	AMX-10	AC	1979
	R-440	SAM	1979
	Mirage F-1A	Fighter	1980
	SA-365N	Hel	1980
	AS-15TT	ASM	1980
	MM-40 Exocet	ShShM	1980
	F-2000 Class	Frigate	1980
	–	Support Ship	1980
	AMX-10P	MICV	1979
	Mirage-4000	Fighter	1981
	OTOMAT-2	ShShM	1980
	Durance class	Support Ship	1980
	AMX-30	AAV	1983
	ATL-2	Mar patrol	1983
	Shahine	SAM	1983
	AMX-30	AAV	1984
	OTOMAT-2	SSHM	1984
	Shahine-2	SAM	1984
	ERC-90	AC	1986
	AS-365	Hel	1985
	ERC-90	AC	1987
UK	FH-70	TH	1981
	Hawk	Trainer/striker	1981
	SNR-6	Hovercraft	1980
	FH-70	TH	1982
	BH-7	Hovercraft	1982
	Hawk	Trainer/striker	1985
	Tornado IDS	Fighter	1985

The economic consequences of the Gulf War

Table 9.10 (continued)

Supplier	Weapon designation	Weapon description	Year of order
	Jetstream 31	Transport	1986
	Tornado ADV	Fighter	1985
	ALARM	ARM	1985
	Sky Flash	AAM	1985
	Hawk	Trainer/striker	1986
	Tornado ADV	Fighter	1986
	Tornado IDS	Fighter	1986
	SSR	Radar	1984
	ALARM	ARM	1986
	Sea Eagle	AShM	1986
	Sky Flash	AAM	1986

Source: SIPRI 1979 to 1987

Table 9.11 Confirmed arms agreements between Saudi Arabia and the major arms suppliers (excluding USA, UK and France), 1979–87

Supplier	Weapon designation	Weapon description	Year of order
Austria	Panzerjager K	TD	1986
Spain	C-212-A	Transport	1984
Austria	Cuirassier	LT, TD	1986
Germany FR	Gepard	AAV	1986
	Leopard-2	MBT	1985
	TP2-1	APC	1982
Italy	VCC-1	APC	1982
Brazil	EE-11 Urutu	APC	1982
Spain	CN-235	Transport	1984
Austria	Cuirassier	LT,TD	1985
Brazil	EE-9	AC	1986
Germany FR	Gepard	AAV	1979
Indonesia	CN-212	Transport	1979
Spain	CN-235	Transport	1985
Austria	Cuirassier	LT, TD	1985
Brazil	EE-T2	MBT	1985
Italy	SH-3D	Hel	1985
Japan	KV-107, 2A	Hel	1982
Switzerland	1 C-9	Trainer	1984
Spain	BMR-600	ICV	1986
Brazil	Astros-11-SS-40	MRS	1985
Germany FR	Wildcat	AAV	1984
Spain	CN-235	Transport	1985
Switzerland	PC-9	Trainer	1985

Note: For meaning of abbreviations, see pp. 155–7.
Source: SIPRI 1979 to 1987

118

Table 9.12 Confirmed arms suppliers to Kuwait, 1979–87

Supplier	Weapon designation	Weapon description	Year of order
France	MM-38 Exocet	ShShM	1978
	MM-40 Exocet	ShShM	1980
	Combattante-2	FAC	1982
	Mirage F-1C	Fighter	1982
	MM-40 Exocet	ShShM/SShM	1982
	AM-39 Exocet	AshM	1983
	AMX-13-90	LT	1983
	AMX-155 MK-F3	SPH	1982
	AS-332	Hel	1983
	Super-530	AAM	1982
	Mirage F-1B	Trainer	1984
	Mirage F-1C	Fighter	1983
	ARMAT	ARM	1983
UK	16M	FPB	1979
	20M	FPB	1979
	Chieftain-5	MBT	1981
	Chieftain-5	MBT	1984
	Hawk	Trainer	1983
	–	LC	1983
	FV-101 Scorpion	LT	1983
	SRM-6	Hovercraft	1980
	–	LC	1984
Germany FR	TNC-45	FPB	1980
	PC-57	PC, FAC	1980
USA	TOW	ATM	1979
	Dhaher	PB	1979
	M-113-A1	ICV	1979
	MIM-23B Hawk	SAM	1979
	M-113-A2	APC	1980
	M-125-A2	APC	1980
	M-577-A2	CPC	1980
	M-901-Tow	ICV	1980
	L-100-30	Transport	1981
	TOW	ATM	1982
	M-113-A2	APC	1982
	TOW	APC	1982
	V-150	APC	1984
	V-300	APC	1984
Soviet Union	SA-7	SAM	1979
	SA-7	SAM	1984
	SA-8	SAM	1984
	Frog-7	SSM	1984

Note: For meanings of abbreviations, see pp. 155–7.
Source: SIPRI 1979 to 1987

Chapter ten

The economic cost of the war: the assignment of a dollar value, September 1980–August 1988

Introduction

In this chapter we will attempt to bring together the various component parts of the economic cost of the war to Iran and Iraq. We will also attempt to assign a dollar value to the war's cost.

Here our task is not simply to add up or compare other estimates that have been made by different economists or research agencies. Indeed, on the contrary, given that this topic has received little attention, we should try to evaluate and use a number of different assumptions and estimating procedures in order to arrive at a figure for the economic cost of the Gulf War.[1]

In all, it should be said that the unavailability of necessary information and data, resulting from eight years of war, has made the task of describing, forecasting or estimating the economic cost of the Iran–Iraq war a daunting assignment indeed.

However, given the available information, we have in this chapter attempted to provide a somewhat detailed estimation of the economic cost of the war. The present study is divided into three parts. The first examines the estimation of the economic cost of the war to Iran, the second estimates Iraq's costs, and the third is an attempt to assess the cost of higher military burdens arising from militarization, in terms of potential foreign-exchange forgone for Iran and Iraq.

The economic cost of the war to Iran

At the outset it should be noted that the Iranian authorities, in contrast to Iraq's, have, from time to time, published their estimates of the economic cost of the war to Iran. However, the estimated cost of the war provided by the Iranian government is most incomplete. Many components of the costs have either wittingly or unwittingly been left out.

Therefore, at this point, an attempt is made to provide the reader with a more comprehensive method of estimating the economic cost of the war.

According to the Iranian authorities, the total economic cost of the war from September 1980 to June 1982 was a total of $150 billion (EIU 1984). Therefore, during the period of 21 months, the monthly cost of the war, on average had amounted to $7.14 billion. This estimated cost does not include oil-revenue losses, although it includes losses incurred in the oil sector. It also includes losses in industry, agriculture, energy, telecommunications, housing and health.

In a second estimate Iran maintained that, by the end of 1984, the total economic cost had increased to $200 billion (based on the same method of estimation) (EIU 1984). This means that, during the 30-month period, June 1982 to December 1984, a further $50 billion of economic losses had been sustained. Therefore, during the second period of the war the losses had declined to $1.7 billion on average each month. However, if the losses are taken as a whole, from September 1980 to December 1984, they amounted to $4.00 billion on average each month.

Finally, in a more recent estimate, according to a Plan and Budget Ministry publication, the economic losses incurred during the first five years of the war had increased to $309 billion (MEED 27 September 1986). This estimate covers a 60-month period, representing a $5.2 billion loss on average per month.

If, at this point, we assume that the economic losses of the war since September 1985 have amounted to an average of $4 billion a month ($4 billion = the average of the three previous estimates), we can note that the estimated economic losses, given Iran's method of estimation, could have increased to $369 billion by the end of 1986.

However, as noted before, the estimates provided by Iran are most incomplete. We now, therefore, attempt to provide a more detailed estimate of the economic cost of the war to Iran from September 1980 to December 1986. To arrive at such an estimate, the following cost elements should be added to the above figure of $369 billion. They are:

1 The cost of 1 million tonnes of oil given to Syria, as a gift, for closing the Iraqi oil pipeline in April 1982 (Stauffer 1985). This means that the period under consideration for our estimation is a total of 57 months. One million tonnes of crude oil a year is equal to 20 thousand barrels a day, and the price of oil per barrel during the period under study being $34 (1982), $29 (1983), $28

(1984), \$28 (1985), \$26 (1986), \$18 (1987) and \$14.6 (1988) means that the total cost to Iran for giving such a gift to Syria, for its support in the war against Iraq, has amounted to \$11 billion.

2 As well as the gift of 1 million tonnes of oil, Iran also agreed to supply Syria with 2.5 million tonnes of crude at a discount of several dollars per barrel. A most quoted discount figure is \$2.0/barrel (Stauffer 1985). Given the volume of oil exports (50 thousand barrels/day) and the rate of discount provided, the total cost to Iran amounts to \$183 million.

3 In the spring of 1984, Iraq started an earnest attack on tanker traffic in the upper region of the Gulf. Between March 1984 and January 1987, 106 tankers carrying Iranian oil were attacked (MEES 6 July 1987). As a result, many ship owners have been reluctant to send their vessels to Kharg Island. Insurance rates for hull and cargo have increased between five and tenfold, so that total shipping rates from Kharg Island have risen from about world scale 20 (before the attacks) to as high as world scale 60–80 (since the attacks). The increase in insurance rates, as well as the increased wage demands by the crew, have resulted in an increase of about \$2 to \$3 per barrel on lifting oil from Kharg Island (Stauffer 1985).

Iran, on the other hand, in order to persuade the ship owners to make the journey through what has become known as 'Exocet Alley' has offered discounts on the price that it charges for its oil, thus reducing its potential foreign-exchange earnings. Therefore, during the period under observation (April 1984 to August 1988), given the volume and price of oil exports, the cost of such a discount has amounted to an estimated total of \$3 billion.

4 Due to sustained Iraqi attacks on oil refineries and oil-production facilities, as well as a reduced level of oil deliveries to the refineries themselves, a general shortage of oil products has been persistent in Iran since the war. Table 10.1 illustrates information on refining capacity, the actual production and domestic consumption of oil products in Iran, during the 1973–86 period.

It can be seen that the refining capacity which had increased from 33,000 thousand tonnes in 1973 to 65,700 thousand tonnes in 1980, has been drastically reduced to only 30,500 thousand tonnes in 1986. However, domestic consumption has increased from 25,254 thousand tonnes in 1980 to 35,950 thousand tonnes in 1986. Because of the inability of refineries to produce enough oil products for domestic consumption, there has been a serious shortage.

Table 10.1 Refining capacity: the actual production of refineries and domestic consumption of oil products, Iran, 1973–86 (thousand tonnes)

	1973	1974	1975	1976	1977	1978	1979	1980	1981	1982	1983	1984	1985	1986
Refining capacity	33,000	34,500	39,500	39,500	47,750	53,800	53,800	65,700	33,000	33,000	33,000	30,500	30,500	30,500
Actual production from refineries	27,735	29,615	32,210	39,965	36,196	33,455	33,005	29,450	31,560	32,781	31,023	31,008	30,357	31,730
Domestic consumption total	12,932	14,760	17,581	21,506	25,311	25,819	26,563	25,254	30,850	35,272	42,621	35,347	35,948	35,950
of which:*														
Petrol	1,426	1,727	2,320	2,737	3,480	3,738	4,210	3,547	3,152	3,358	4,410	4,303	+	+
Kerosene	3,145	3,653	3,690	5,026	5,811	4,795	5,924	4,700	4,470	5,382	6,933	5,918	+	+
Diesel oil	3,932	4,407	5,346	6,259	7,552	5,351	8,178	8,048	12,798	10,062	12,041	11,218	+	+
Fuel oils	3,808	4,205	4,883	5,467	5,919	8,984	6,173	6,908	8,426	8,335	9,604	12,492	+	+
Production less consumption	14,803	14,855	14,629	18,459	10,885	7,636	6,442	4,198	710	−2,491	−11,598	−4,339	−5,591	−4,220
	(298)	(299)	(295)	(372)	(219)	(154)	(130)	(85)	(14)	(−50)	(−234)	(−87)	(−113)	(−85)

Notes: * Due to rounding, it may not add up to total.
    + Not known.
    ( ) The figures in brackets represent one thousand barrels per day. They have been computed by the author using the following: 1 tonne = 7.33 barrels.
Sources: Statistiques 1981, 1982, 1983, 1986

It can be seen that by 1982 Iran had turned into a net importer of oil products, importing 50 thousand barrels/day that year, and more in subsequent years. In order to estimate the cost of oil product imports to Iran, we obviously have to know the price per barrel of different oil products, exported to Iran. However, it seems that a wall of secrecy surrounds this issue, as no oil company that we approached was prepared to supply us with the required information.

However, in 1987, a contract with the Soviet Union for imports of 2 million tonnes of refined oil products by Iran in exchange for 5 million tonnes of crude export to that country was signed (MEED 31 October 1987). Does this mean that the price for oil products is generally 2.5 times the price of crude? If this was to be the case, then the cost of oil-product imports to Iran during the period under study is an estimated total of $14 billion.

Another economic cost of the war is the potential loss in export of oil products by Iran. However, the lack of information and data precludes the possibility of even trying to estimate this potential loss. None the less, as most of Abadan's output was for the export market, the loss in foreign-exchange earnings could be substantial.

5 At the outset of the war, the port facilities at Khoramshahr and Abadan were destroyed. This forced Iran to shift its imports to other smaller, less efficient ports, and also to direct more of its imports by rail and road links through the Soviet Union and Turkey. Table 10.2 provides information on the weight of commodities (excluding oil products) unloaded at commercial ports during the 1978–84 period.

Table 10.2 Weight of commodities (excluding oil products) unloaded at commercial ports, 1978–84 (thousand tonnes)

Port	1978	1979	1980	1981	1982	1983	1984
Khorramshahr	3,641	1,278	856	0	0	0	0
Imam Khomeini	5,833	4,019	4,106	3,466	2,137	3,803	2,284
Anzali	385	395	561	519	803	839	508
Bushehr	696	354	524	748	1,250	2,024	1,095
Bandar-e-Abbas and Bandar-e-Shahid Rajavi	2,983	2,335	3,734	6,248	5,684	7,575	6,735
Nowshahr	117	91	166	207	177	303	170
Abadan	881	301	75	0	0	0	0
Chahbahar	X	X	X	X	X	428	502
Total	14,536	8,773	10,022	11,183	10,051	14,972	11,294

Note: X Negligible.
Sources: Statistical Centre of Iran 1986, 1987

It can be seen that in 1980 (9 months), Khoramshahr and Abadan had handled 856 thousand tonnes and 75 thousand tonnes of imports respectively. Since the war no cargo has arrived at these ports which originally had better links with markets. Moreover, since 1980, there has been a significant rate of increase in imports at Bushehr and Bandar-e-Abbas and Bandar-e-Shahid Rajavi. More recently, there has also been some development at Chahbahar to enable it to handle more of Iran's imports (see further table 10.2).

The changes in ports handling imports as well as the higher rate of insurance premiums for shipping in the Gulf in general have resulted in an extra freight cost of $30–50 per ton of imports (Stauffer 1985). As noted in table 10.2, the total imports were 10,022 thousand tonnes in 1980 (12 months). Therefore, the total imports for the last quarter of the year (i.e. since the war) amounted to 2,506 thousand tonnes. The corresponding figures for the whole of 1981 were (11,183 thousand tonnes), 1982 (10,051 thousand tonnes), 1983 (14,972 thousand tonnes) and 1984 (11,294 thousand tonnes). Given the overall reduction in imports since 1983, it is most likely that the volume of imports has declined to about 10 million tonnes per year during the 1985–6 period.

If, at this point, the above figures are multiplied by $40/tonne (which is the middle point between the lower and upper bounds of extra freight charges), we will arrive at the figure of $3.5 billion, which represents the estimated extra cost of importing since the war.

6 As will be demonstrated in more detail later in this chapter, where the opportunity cost of the militarization of Iran and Iraq is the subject of study, the total actual military expenditure (Milex) in Iran during the 1981–6 period (i.e. since the war) has amounted to $86.5 billion. We have also shown that, given the revolutionary government's desire for maintaining a 4.5 per cent defence burden, the potential Milex during the same period could have been $37 billion.

The difference between the actual and potential Milex is $49.5 billion. This sum could, for example, have been invested abroad. It it had, given the actual interest rates during the same period, then by the end of 1986 its compounded value could have increased to the total of $76.1 billion. Therefore, another economic cost of the war is the loss of this potential earning. Given the actual Milex during the 1986–8 period, as well as our method of estimation of the potential Milex, as noted above, this means that the potential foreign exchange losses had increased to $84 billion by August 1988.

At this point, if all the above figures are combined we will arrive at the semi-grand total economic cost of the war of $560.7 billion. However, in order to arrive at the grand total cost, the oil revenue losses should also be included.

The estimation of oil revenue losses in Iran since the war, it seems, is an impossible task, as the country's oil production/exports were much disrupted well before the war. However, at this point, an attempt is made to provide an educated guess concerning the estimation of the potential oil-revenue losses resulting from the war.

Table 10.3 provides information on such estimation. The table first notes the actual total oil exports and revenues during the 1980–6 period. They were 446,815 thousand tonnes and $91.5 billion.

Table 10.3 Estimation of potential oil revenue, Iran, 1980–6

	Actual oil prices per barrel US $	Actual oil exports (thousand tonnes)	Actual oil revenues bn. rials and, in brackets, in bn. US $	Potential oil exports* (thousand tonnes)	Potential oil revenue* bn. rials and, in brackets, in bn. US $
1980	32	40,112	684 (9.7)	53,482	886 (12.5)
1981	37	41,079	732 (9.3)	54,771	1,163 (14.8)
1982	34	81,724	1,508 (18.1)	108,963	2,270 (27.1)
1983	29	81,100	1,621 (18.8)	124,980	2,295 (26.6)
1984	28	72,600	1,066 (11.8)	129,229	2,387 (26.5)
1985	28	72,100	1,157 (12.7)	129,229	2,387 (26.5)
1986	26	58,100	873 (11.1)	138,404	2,079 (26.4)
Total		446,815	7,641 (91.5)	739,058	13,467 (160.5)

Note: * Author's estimation.
Sources: For actual figures: IMFa 1987 and *Statistiques* 1980 to 1986

In order to arrive at the potential oil exports, we assumed that for 1980, the actual and potential oil exports were the same, except that during the last quarter of the year oil exports were severely disrupted. Therefore, 13,370 thousand tonnes of oil was added to the volume of actual oil exports in 1980 to arrive at the figure of 53,482 thousand tonnes, representing the potential oil exports for the same year.

To estimate the potential oil exports for 1981 and 1982, we assumed that they would have grown at the same rate at which the actual oil exports had grown, i.e. at 2.4 and 98.0 per cent during the 1980–1 and 1981–2 periods.

From 1982 onwards, the oil prices started to fall. This coincided with a serious oil glut that had developed earlier. At this point, we assumed that pragmatism would have prevailed in Iran, and that the authorities would have increased the volume of oil exports only by the rate at which oil prices were falling.

If this scenario was to have been adopted, then, as oil prices fell by 14.7 per cent during the 1982–3 period, oil exports would have increased at the same rate, to 124,980 thousand tonnes in 1983. The same line of reasoning was applied to our estimation of oil revenue losses for the rest of the period under study. Having estimated these figures and multiplied them by the oil prices, we were able to estimate the potential oil-revenue losses. In our estimation, we have used the actual oil prices; to do otherwise would have meant estimating the potential oil prices. This would have made our task even more daunting than it already is. In order to avoid the usage of so many unknown figures we decided to use the actual oil prices.

In all, during the 1980–6 period, the potential oil revenues could have been a total of $160.4 billion. Therefore, the total potential loss in oil revenues since the war is the estimated sum of $69.0 billion. The actual oil revenues during the last 17 months of the war were $14.2 billion. Thus, the total actual oil revenue during the war period is $105.7 billion. Therefore, the total potential oil revenue losses since the war (given our assumptions) is $83.6 billion.

If the above figure is added to the semi-grand sum of $560.7 billion, we will arrive at the grand total economic cost of $644.3 billion. This sum, represents only the monetary cost of the war to Iran. It does not include inflationary costs, the loss of services and earnings by the many hundreds of thousands of people killed, the depletion of national resources, the postponement of crucial development projects, the cost of the delayed training and education of the young people, and finally the figure also excludes the cost of welfare payments to the hundreds of thousands injured in the war who are not able to contribute fully in the creation of wealth for the national economy.

The economic cost of the war to Iraq

The Iraqi government, in contrast to Iran's, has not published any estimates of the economic cost of the war. This makes the task of estimating such a cost to Iraq's economy a very complicated assignment indeed.

In order to arrive at the value of the economic cost to Iraq, the following components should be identified: the estimated cost of damages inflicted upon the infrastructure; the estimated oil revenue losses; and the estimated GNP losses.

Then the combined figure of the above costs should be added to any other component parts of the economic costs in order to arrive at the grand total economic cost of the war to Iraq. The period under consideration for our estimation is the same period as in the case of Iran, from September 1980 to August 1988, or a total of 84 months.

Estimating the cost of damages to the infrastructure

In order to arrive at this estimated cost, the following was assumed. We argue that, because of Iran's less efficient air force, it has not been possible to carry out many bombing missions and inflict serious damage throughout the war period. Furthermore most of the damage on the infrastructure was sustained during the early months of the conflict.

Since then, air and missile attacks against cities and other economic targets in Iraq have been very sporadic. Given this observation, therefore, the monthly cost to Iraq can be assumed to be much less than that sustained by Iran. We assume that the average economic loss to Iraq's economy during the period under study to be $0.8 billion each month, as compared to Iran's $4.9 billion. Therefore the total cost of damage to Iraq's infrastructure since the war and up to August 1988 is the sum of $67.0 billion. This cost does not include oil-revenue losses, although it includes losses incurred in the oil sector. It also includes losses in industry, agriculture, energy, telecommunications, housing and health.

Estimating oil-revenue losses

Table 10.4 provides information for estimating potential oil exports and revenue during the 1980–6 period. In order to gauge the potential oil revenue during the period under study, we took the actual figure for 1980 (for the first 9 months of the year only), assumed that exports would have continued at the same rate for the last 3 months of the year and added to it the figure of 40,133 thousand tonnes to arrive at the potential oil export figure.

Therefore the potential oil exports for 1980, given our assumption, is a total of 160,533 thousand tonnes. For 1981 we assumed that Iraq's oil exports would have grown at the same rate as Iran's potential exports, that is at 2.4 per cent. Therefore, by 1981, Iraq's potential oil exports would have increased to 164,386 thousand tonnes.

Table 10.4   Estimation of potential oil revenue, Iraq, 1980–6

	Actual oil prices per barrel US $	Actual oil exports (thousand tonnes)	Actual oil revenues bn. dinars and, in brackets, in bn. US $	Potential oil exports* (thousand tonnes)	Potential oil revenue* bn. dinars and, in brackets, in bn. US $
1980	32	120,400	7,718 (22.4)	160,533	10,291 (29.8)
1981	37	34,100	3,068 (8.9)	164,386	12,934 (44.6)
1982	34	39,300	3,014 (9.3)	164,386	13,287 (41.0)
1983	29	32,500	3,000 (9.3)	183,290	12,903 (40.0)
1984	28	33,500	3,495 (10.8)	183,290	12,168 (37.6)
1985	28	48,549	3,862 (11.9)	183,290	12,168 (37.6)
1986	26	62,100	3,782 (12.1)	183,290	10,908 (34.9)
Total		370,449	27,939 (84.7)	1,222,465	84,659 (265.5)

Note: * Author's estimation.
Sources: For actual figures: IMFa 1987 and *Statistiques* 1980 to 1986

In 1982, however, Iran's potential oil exports, as noted above, had increased to 108,963 thousand tonnes, a figure which was only 12,224 thousand tonnes less than the actual oil exports in 1979. Given this, we argue that Iraq would have found it difficult to increase its oil exports further. Therefore, for 1982, it is probable that Iraq would have kept its oil exports at the 1981 level.

However, in 1983, oil prices fell to $29/barrel. This represents a decline of 11.5 per cent since 1981. Given such a fall in oil prices, we then assume that Iraq would have increased its oil exports by 11.5 per cent in order to maintain its financial position. So for 1983, the potential oil exports would have increased to 183,290 thousand tonnes. This figure is by far the largest volume of oil exports, when compared with Iraq's historical actual exports. The highest volume of actual oil exports was in 1979 when they reached 160,400 thousand tonnes.

Therefore, at this point we assume that by 1983, Iraq's potential oil exports had reached a point where a higher output had become very difficult to achieve. Therefore, in our estimation, we have said that, from 1983 onwards, Iraq's potential oil exports would have remained the same, at 183,290 thousand tonnes/annum for 1984, 1985 and 1986. We then noted that Iraq's potential oil revenue during the 1980–6 period would have been a total of $265.5 billion. By comparing this figure with the actual total revenue during the same period, we arrive at an estimated total lost revenue of $180.0 billion. The actual oil revenues for the last 17 months of the war were $17.3 billion. Therefore, the total

potential losses in oil revenues during the entire war period is
$197.7 billion (given our assumptions).

Estimating GNP losses

In addition to the cost elements for infrastructure damage and oil-
revenue losses, we should also add to the cost of the war that part
of the national output which would have been produced if Iraq's
economy had not been severely disrupted as a result of the war.
Similar calculations for Iran were not necessary, since such GNP
loss had already been included by the Iranian government in its
own estimates of the cost of the war to Iran's economy.

Table 10.5 provides information on the estimation of Iraq's
potential GNP during the 1980–6 period. In order to estimate the
potential GNP, we first looked at the relationship between actual
oil revenue and GNP during the 1976–80 period. It was noted that
during this period on average each year oil revenue had accounted
for 50 per cent of the GNP figures.

Table 10.5 Estimation of Iraq's potential GNP, 1980–6

	Actual GNP	Potential GNP*
1980	15.8 (45.8)	20.6 (59.7)
1981	11.1 (32.2)	25.9 (75.1)
1982	12.6 (39.1)	26.6 (82.5)
1983	13.1 (40.6)	25.8 (80.0)
1984	13.9 (43.1)	24.3 (75.3)
1985	16.8 (52.1)	24.3 (75.3)
1986	17.1ᵉ (54.7)	21.8 (69.8)
Total	100.4 (306.7)	169.3 (518.5)

Notes: * and ᵉ Author's estimation. The actual and potential GNP figures are in billion current
  Iraqi dinars and the figures (in brackets) are their equivalent in billion US $.
Sources: IMFa 1987 and March 1988 and United Nations Economic Commission for Western
  Asia 1986b

We then said that, in the absence of war, Iraq's potential oil
revenue would again have accounted for 50 per cent of the
country's potential GNP. We were then able to calculate the
potential GNP figures. Thus, we arrived at the total potential GNP
figure of $518.5 billion. The actual total GNP figure during the
same period is $307.6 billion. The difference between these two
($210.9 billion) is that part of the national output which could have
been produced if Iraq was not at war. During the last 17 months of
the war the actual GNP was $79.7 billion, while the potential
figure (given our assumptions) could have been $90.0 billion.

Therefore, the total estimated losses in GNP during the war period are $222.1 billion.

However, in order to avoid double counting, we should subtract from the $222.1 billion loss of GNP, the $197.7 billion loss of potential oil revenue. By doing so, we will arrive at the figure of $24.4 billion which is considered to be the output lost because of the war above and beyond lost oil revenue.

At this point, if the estimated cost components (infrastructure, oil revenue, GNP) are added together, we will arrive at the semi-grand total economic cost of the war to Iraq, $289.1 billion. However, in order to arrive at a more comprehensive figure of the grand total economic cost, the following various cost elements should be added:

1 As was noted before, at the start of the war Iraq had accumulated $35 billion in foreign-exchange reserves. By the second or third year of the war the foreign reserves had been totally depleted. Hence a major economic consequence of the war must be the almost complete erosion of the country's foreign reserves. If this sum, namely the original $35 billion, had been kept in overseas banks and had been allowed to receive a compounded interest, by the end of the war, Iraq's foreign exchange reserves would have increased to $78.8 billion.[2]

   This sum does not take into consideration the possibility that, indeed, Iraq might have been able to increase its original foreign-exchange reserves. Given our estimation of Iraq's potential oil revenue since 1980, it is most likely that in the absence of the war, Iraq by now could have become another Kuwait, with massive foreign-exchange reserves.[3]

2 Iraq is landlocked, except for a very narrow outlet on to the uppermost end of the Gulf. None the less, Iraq had traditionally relied upon the sea for its imports. However, at the very early stages of the war Basrah, the main port, and the smaller port, Fao, were put out of action.

   The serious disruption at Basrah and Fao meant that Iraq had to find other routes for transporting its imports. Here the assistance given to Iraq by its Arab neighbours has proved invaluable. Not only have they financed some of Iraq's imports, but they have also opened their ports to Iraq-bound shipping. Certain quays at Shuaiba, Shuwaikh and Damman have been put aside to handle Iraqi-bound cargoes. Jordan has also worked out special arrangements with Iraq. The port of Aqaba has been put at Iraq's disposal. Finally, Turkey, on a purely commercial basis, has permitted a greatly expanded overland truck traffic across Anatolia to Iraq (Stauffer 1985).

It is estimated that the above changes in import routes have added an extra cost of $600 million on average each year to Iraq's import bill since the war (Stauffer 1985). Therefore another component part of the economic cost to Iraq is the sum of $4.7 billion.

3 As will be demonstrated later, the total actual military expenditure (Milex) in Iraq during the 1981–6 period (i.e. since the war) has amounted to $60.6 billion. However, based on an action–reaction model, and given the reduction in Iran's defence burden to 4.5 per cent soon after the revolution, it is possible to argue that Iraq's total potential Milex could have been $20.6 billion (based on a 4.5 per cent defence burden on average each year). The difference between the above two figures ($40.0 billion) is the military cost of the war. If this sum had been invested overseas, then by the end of 1986 its compounded value would have been $50.7 billion. Given the actual Milex during the last 17 months of the war and the potential Milex (given our assumptions), it is possible to argue that the difference between these two figures by the end of the war could have increased to $55.3 billion, which in fact is the military cost of the war to Iraq. If this sum had been invested overseas, then by July 1988 its compounded value would have been $80 billion. This sum represents another item of the economic cost of the war.

At this point, if all the component parts of the economic cost to Iraq's economy are added together, we will arrive at the grand total cost of $452.6 billion. If the figures of the economic cost of the war to Iran and Iraq are compared, it can be seen that, in the case of Iran the total cost includes more actual cost, while in the case of Iraq it includes more opportunity cost. This is because in the case of Iran, we assumed a much higher rate of actual damage inflicted on the infrastructure. The difference in the size of the different cost components for estimating the economic cost of the war can best be seen in figure 10.1 which illustrates the cost components of the war to Iran and Iraq.

At this point it should be noted that, in line with the policy adopted by other economists and research institutions that have estimated the cost of other wars such as Vietnam (Stevens 1986), we too have made no attempt to estimate the cost of the Gulf War in constant prices. To have done so – if it were at all possible, given the many different cost components that we have used – would have produced a 'hodge podge' – to quote Robert Warren Stevens (1986) – of price- and time-adjusted figures that could have been compared only with great difficulty and confusion with one another and with readily available published figures.[4]

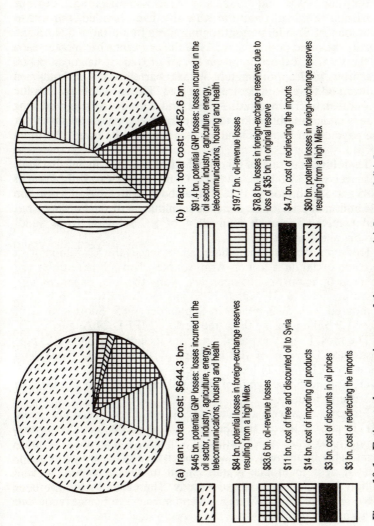

(a) Iran: total cost: $644.3 bn.

$445 bn. potential GNP losses: losses incurred in the oil sector, industry, agriculture, energy, telecommunications, housing and health

$84 bn. potential losses in foreign-exchange reserves resulting from a high Milex

$83.6 bn. oil-revenue losses

$11 bn. cost of free and discounted oil to Syria

$14 bn. cost of importing oil products

$3 bn. cost of discounts in oil prices

$3 bn. cost of redirecting the imports

(b) Iraq: total cost: $452.6 bn.

$91.4 bn. potential GNP losses: losses incurred in the oil sector, industry, agriculture, energy, telecommunications, housing and health

$197.7 bn. oil-revenue losses

$78.8 bn. losses in foreign-exchange reserves due to loss of $35 bn. in original reserve

$4.7 bn. cost of redirecting the imports

$80 bn. potential losses in foreign-exchange reserves resulting from a high Milex

Figure 10.1 Estimated economic cost of the war to (a) Iran and (b) Iraq

To return to our original discussion a further serious consquence of the war for Iraq's economy, especially for the future, is the rise in Iraq's international indebtedness.

As noted above, on the eve of the war, Iraq had $35 billion in foreign-exchange reserves. However, by the first quarter of 1987, Iraq had accumulated debts of between $50 and $80 billion. The largest portion of the total debt is owed to Saudi Arabia and Kuwait.

Between 1980 and 1982, the Arab supporters of Iraq, in particular the Saudis and the Kuwaitis, had provided Iraq with a cash loan of $1 billion/month, amounting to a total of $24 billion during the same period. Since 1982 the assistance has mostly been in the form of exporting oil on behalf of Iraq. It has been noted that from 1982 approximately 300,000 barrels a day of Saudi and Kuwaiti oil have been dedicated to Iraq. This oil is sold by Iraq for physical delivery by Saudi Arabia and Kuwait. It is agreed that Iraq is under an obligation to repay these volumes of oil as well as the payment of loans in kind at some point in the future (Stauffer 1976).

Therefore, the sale of oil on behalf of Iraq has meant that Iraq has received $3.7 billion in 1983, $3.5 billion in 1984, $3.2 billion in 1985 and $2.9 billion in 1986. If the above figures are added to the $24 billion of cash loans, it can be seen that by the end of 1986 Iraq had received the cash equivalent of $37.3 billion from Saudi Arabia and Kuwait.

However, of more immediate significance is the $20 billion or so in commercial debt to non-Arab sources. Not all these debts are covered by export-credit agencies. None the less, exposure with these agencies at 31 March 1987 was increased to $11.6 billion, compared with $9.3 billion in September 1985. Short-term debt was $1.9 billion during the same period (MEED 29 August 1987).

The most heavily exposed countries include Japan. The Export Insurance Division of the Ministry of International Trade and Industry (EID/MITI) has a total exposure of $2.4 billion. Moreover, around 50 per cent of the total exposure is in the form of short-term loans.

France is another major creditor of Iraq. However, unlike EID/MITI, the bulk of the French export-credit agency Cofac's exposure to Iraq, which totals $2.3 billion, is medium- and long-term. This figure includes only the civilian debt. Iraq's military-related debt to France is understood to have increased to $3.7 billion during the period under study. Therefore, by the spring of 1987, the total Iraqi debt (civilian and military) to France amounted to $6 billion.

Italy's export-credit agency, SACE, reported a total exposure of $2.4 billion at the end of 1986. According to the West German export-credit agency, Hermes, their total exposure by 31 December 1986, had increased to $1.8 billion. Debt owed to the UK is mostly medium-term debt, and by early 1987 had increased to about $1.2 billion (MEED 29 August 1987).

The countries mentioned above (excluding the UK) have to some extent limited their export-credit agencies in the granting of credit to Iraq. However, two Western countries, the UK and the USA, have adopted a more flexible attitude to Baghdad's payment problems and continue to provide funding to Iraq. The UK has arranged for a short-term credit facility to provide loans of $50 million at a time to Baghdad (MEED 29 August 1987).

Eximbank of the US has arranged for 180-day transactions, limited to international letters of credit issued by the Central Bank of Iraq. Eximbank apart, the US is one of Baghdad's most crucial sources of funding through its agricultural-credit programme. This type of credit allows Iraq to import a wide range of produce. The programme has provided Iraq with an allocation of $573 million in 1987, up from $500 million in 1986. The additional allocation for 1987 includes financing for freight charges. Iraq is the only country to receive such assistance from the USA (MEED 29 August 1987).

At this point, if the grand total economic costs of the war to both countries (the total of $644.3 billion for Iran and $452.6 billion for Iraq) are combined, then we will arrive at the grand total economic cost of the war to both countries: $1,097.0 billion. This figure, which should be read as 1 trillion, and 97 billion dollars, is indeed a mind-boggling sum.

To put the total economic cost of the war in meaningful perspective, it suffices to say that the cost of the war exceeds the total oil revenue which Iran and Iraq have received throughout this century. From 1919 to July 1988 in Iran's case, and from 1931 to the same period in the case of Iraq, the total joint oil revenues earned is the sum of $418.5 billion. That is, the cost of the war exceeded by $678.5 billion the entire revenue from oil ever since the two countries started to sell their oil on the world market. If the cost of the war is related to their GNP, it can be seen that, on average each year, the cost of the war has absorbed 60 per cent of Iran's and 112 per cent of Iraq's GNP during the 1980–8 period.

Table 10.6 The opportunity cost of Iran's military expenditure (Milex) in terms of foreign–exchange reserves forgone,[a] through inability to keep a 4.5 per cent defence burden each year, 1981–6

	Actual GDP	Actual Milex A	Actual share of Milex in GDP %	Milex could have been, if 4.5% defence burden each year B	Sums could have been available for investment abroad [A–B]	US certificate-of-deposit rate %	Foreign-exchange reserves, including interests earned (compounded)
1981	8,218	1,007 (12.9)	12.3	370 (4.7)	(8.2)	15.91	(9.0)
1982	10,621	1,300 (15.5)	12.3	478 (5.7)	(9.8)	12.35	(20.6)
1983	13,471	1,500 (17.4)	11.1	606 (7.0)	(10.4)	9.09	(32.3)
1984	15,030	1,833 (20.4)	12.3	676 (7.5)	(12.9)	10.37	(50.6)
1985	15,306	1,295 (14.2)	8.5	689 (7.5)	(6.7)	8.05	(71.3)
1986	15,609[b]	482 (6.1)	8.0	356 (4.5)	(1.6)	6.8	(76.1)

Notes: [a] Author's calculation.
[b] Author's estimation. Figures quoted are in billion current rials, except those in brackets which are in current billion dollars.
Sources: IMFa 1987; IISS 1979/80 to 1987/8

Table 10.7 The opportunity cost of Iraq's military expenditures (Milex) in terms of foreign-exchange reserves forgone,[a] through inability to keep Milex at 4.5 per cent of GDP each year, 1981–6

	Actual GDP	Actual Milex	Actual share of Milex in GDP (%)	Potential GDP	Potential Milex, if Milex = 4.5% of GDP each year	Sums could have been available for investment abroad	US certificate-of-deposit rate (%)	Foreign exchange reserves, including interests earned (compounded)
		A		B		[A–B]		
1981	11.1	1.4 (4.7)	12.6	25.9	1.2 (3.4)	(1.3)	15.91	(1.5)
1982	12.6	2.4 (7.7)	19.0	26.6	1.2 (3.7)	(4.0)	12.35	(6.2)
1983	13.1	3.2 (10.2)	24.0	25.8	1.2 (3.6)	(6.6)	9.09	(13.9)
1984	13.9	4.3 (13.7)	31.0	24.3	1.1 (3.4)	(10.3)	10.37	(26.8)
1985	16.6	4.0 (12.7)	25.0	24.3	1.1 (3.4)	(9.3)	8.05	(39.0)
1986	17.1[b]	3.7 (11.6)	21.6	21.8	1.0 (3.1)	(8.5)	6.8	(50.7)

Notes: [a] Author's calculation.
[b] Author's estimation. Figures quoted are in billion current dinars, except those in brackets which are in current billion dollars.
Sources: IMFa 1987; IISS 1979/80 and 1987/8; and United Nations Economic and Social Commission for Western Asia 1986a

Estimating the military cost of the war (1981–6) as well as the opportunity cost of the militarization of Iran and Iraq: 1973–75.

At this point an attempt is made to assess the cost of high military burdens arising from militarization, in terms of potential foreign-exchange reserves forgone, for Iran and Iraq. The underlying assumptions in our estimate are the same as those given in chapter nine.

However, before estimating the opportunity cost of militarization, we will first attempt to estimate the military cost of the war to Iran and Iraq, whose figures were noted on pages 125 and 132. The underlying assumption in all the estimates here is that a 4.5 per cent defence burden has been operational during the period under study in all of the countries under observation. The potential and actual Milex will then be compared. The changes that occur are in a sense the opportunity costs.

Table 10.6 illustrates the opportunity cost of Iran's Milex in terms of foreign-exchange reserves forgone as a result of not being able to keep to a 4.5 per cent defence burden each year during the 1981–6 period. The corresponding information for Iraq is provided in table 10.7.

It can be seen that the total actual Milex in Iran during the 1981–6 period (i.e. since the war) has amounted to $86.5 billion. However, if Iran had maintained a 4.5 per cent defence burden, its potential Milex could have been $37 billion during the same period. The difference between the actual and potential Milex ($49.5 billion) is the opportunity cost of the increased defence burden since 1981. This sum also represents the military cost of the war to Iran (i.e. $37 billion is the total Milex that Iran would have spent in the absence of the war).

Furthermore, if the above $49.5 billion had been invested abroad, then, by the end of 1986, its compounded value (given our assumption) could have increased to $76.1 billion.

Iraq's total actual Milex since the war has amounted to $60.6 billion. (This sum does not include the financial assistance provided by the Gulf Co-operation Council to Iraq). Given the potential GDP/Milex, Iraq's potential military expenditure could have amounted to $20.6 billion (given our assumption). The difference between these two figures ($40.0 billion) is the military cost of the war to Iraq.

Moreover, if the above figure was invested abroad, by the end of 1986, its potential value could have increased to a total of $50.7 billion. Therefore, if Iran and Iraq were not at war, and had kept to a 4.5 per cent defence burden each year, together they could have accumulated a golden sum of $126.7 billion in foreign-exchange reserves during the 1981–6 period.

Moreover, from tables 10.8 and 9 at the end of this chapter, it can be seen that, if both Iran and Iraq had maintained a 4.5 per cent defence burden since the first oil-price increase of the 1973/4 period, they could have accumulated $133.2 billion and $62.4 billion in foreign-exchange reserves during the 1973–85 period respectively. At this point, if the estimated figures for the potential foreign-exchange reserve losses for Saudi Arabia and Kuwait (which were noted in chapter nine) are added to those of Iran and Iraq's, we will arrive at the grand total figure of $436.3 billion, which these four countries could have accumulated between themselves, given our assumptions.

Now the reader is invited to compare this potential loss with the potential gains that could have been possible, if the above sum had, for example, been invested for Third World Development under the supervision of the potential Gulf World Development Bank that could have been established by the above countries. Food for thought, we hope.

Conclusion

In this chapter we attempted to bring together the various component parts of the economic cost of the war to Iran and Iraq. The estimated opportunity cost of the militarization of both countries in terms of foreign-exchange reserves forgone was also noted.

Given our assumptions, we estimated that the total economic cost of the war to Iran, from 1980 to 1986, is the total of $644.3 billion. The corresponding figure for Iraq is $452.6 billion. The above sums represent only the monetary cost of the war to both countries. They do not include inflationary costs, the loss of services and earnings by the many hundreds of thousands of people killed, the depletion of natural resources, the postpone-ment of crucial development projects, the cost of delayed training and education of the young people and finally too the figures do not include the cost of welfare payments to the hundreds of thousands injured in the war who are not able to contribute fully to the creation of wealth for the national economy.

This chapter also noted that, although the total economic cost of the war to Iran and Iraq's economies are very close, none the less a major difference exists in the way they were arrived at. That is, in the case of Iran the total cost includes more actual costs, while in the case of Iraq its total includes more opportunity costs. This was because in the case of Iran a much higher rate of actual damage to the infrastructure was assumed.

We also noted that the grand total economic cost of the war to both countries together is the sum of $1,097 billion. In order to put this figure into better perspective, we noted that this figure exceeds by $678.5 billion the entire oil revenue received by both countries ever since they started to sell their oil on the world market, a mind-boggling price to be paid for the execution of war by any standards.

The chapter also noted that the military cost of the war to Iran during the 1981–8 period (given our assumption) is the sum of $49.5 billion. The corresponding figure for Iraq is $55.3 billion.

It was also argued that, if Iran and Iraq had agreed on a 4.5 per cent defence burden since 1973, then, by 1986, they could have accumulated a combined sum of nearly $196 billion in foreign-exchange reserves, a substantial sum of money by any standard. We also noted that the combined foreign-exchange reserve losses for Iran, Iraq, Saudi Arabia and Kuwait, during the 1973–85 period, by not maintaining a 4.5 per cent defence burden each year has amounted to $436.3 billion.

It was argued that, if the above potential loss had been turned into a potential gain (i.e. by maintaining a 4.5 per cent defence burden), then the above sum, for example, could have been turned into capital for the establishment of the potential Gulf World Development Bank to foster and promote development projects in the Third World.

Table 10.8 The opportunity cost of Iran's military expenditures (Milex) in terms of foreign-exchange reserves forgone,* through inability to keep Milex at 4.5 per cent of the GDP each year, 1973–85

	Actual GDP	Actual Milex	Actual share of Milex in GDP	Milex should have been, given our assumptions (4.5% of GDP/year)	Sums could have been available for investment abroad, given our assumptions [A–B]	US certificate-of-deposit rate (%)	Foreign-exchange reserves, including interests earned (compounded)	Foreign-exchange Equivalent in bn. US $
		A	A	B				
1973	1,784	145	8.1	80	65	6.95	–	–
1974	3,072	218	7.1	138	80	7.82	69.5	1.02
1975	3,479	707	20.3	156	551	7.49	161.2	2.4
1976	4,480	665	14.8	202	463	6.77	765.5	10.9
1977	5,207	561	10.8	234	327	6.69	1,311.7	18.5
1978	4,917	693	14.1	221	472	8.29	1,748.3	24.6
1979	6,053	278	4.5	278	–	11.2	2,355.6	33.2
1980	6,759	317	4.7	304	13	13.07	2,619.4	38.9
1981	8,218	1,007	12.3	370	637	15.91	2,976.5	30.2
1982	10,621	1,300	12.3	478	822	12.35	4,188.4	49.9
1983	13,471	1,500	11.1	606	894	9.09	5,629.2	65.5
1984	15,030	1,833	12.3	676	1,157	10.37	7,116.2	79.1
1985	15,306	1,295	8.5	689	606	8.05	9,131.1	100.3
1986							10,520.9	133.2

Notes: * Author's calculation. All the figures quoted – except where otherwise indicated – are in current billion rials.
Sources: Central Bank of Iran, Annual Report and Balance Sheet, 1349, 1351, 1359, 1362; IMFa 1986 and August 1987; and IISS, 1975/76 to 1986/7

Table 10.9 The opportunity cost of Iraq's military expenditures (Milex) in terms of foreign-exchange reserves forgone* through inability to keep Milex at 4.5 per cent of GDP each year, 1973–85

	Actual GDP	Actual Milex A	Actual share of Milex in GDP	Milex should have been, given our assumptions (4.5% of GDP/year) our assumptions B	Sums could have been available for investment abroad, given [A–B]	US certificate-of-deposit rate (%)	Foreign-exchange Equivalent reserves, including interests earned (compounded)	in bn. US $
1973	1.6	0.165	10.9	0.072	0.093	6.95	—	—
1974	3.4	0.236	6.9	0.153	0.083	7.82	0.182	0.61
1975	4.0	0.356	8.9	0.018	0.176	7.49	0.372	1.28
1976	5.2	0.394	7.6	0.234	0.160	6.77	0.600	2.01
1977	5.9	0.492	8.3	0.266	0.226	6.69	0.867	3.00
1978	7.0	0.586	8.4	0.315	0.271	8.29	1.12	3.86
1979	11.4	0.789	6.9	0.513	0.276	11.22	1.495	5.17
1980	15.8	0.879	5.6	0.711	0.168	13.07	1.831	6.20
1981	11.1	1.4	12.6	1.2	0.2	15.91	2.971	10.0
1982	12.6	2.4	19.0	1.2	1.2	12.35	5.276	17.10
1983	13.1	3.2	24.4	1.2	2.0	9.09	8.539	27.41
1984	13.9	4.3	31.0	1.1	3.1	10.37	13.267	42.90
1985	16.8	4.0	25.0	1.1	2.9	8.05	17.895	57.74
1986							19.335	62.37

Notes: * Author's calculation. The figures quoted are all in bn current Iraqi dinars except those in column (8).
Sources: IMFa 1980, 1982 and 1986; OPEC 1985; and IISS 1973/74 to 1986/87. Yearbooks

Chapter eleven

Conclusion

In this book an attempt has been made to analyse the economic consequences of the war on Iran and Iraq. This final chapter not only summarizes the conclusions to the previous chapters, but also tries to put forward some recommendations concerning post-war reconstruction. In this chapter we will also identify the measures that must be introduced by the countries concerned in order to bring about long-term peace and security in the region.

The chapter is therefore divided into three parts. The first summarizes the conclusions to the chapters. From the account of the destruction caused by the war, it becomes clear that both Iran and Iraq, sooner or later, must start the gigantic task of reconstruction and development. Therefore, in the second part, some aspects of the nature of the reconstruction process, its stages and the possible strategies will be noted.

No attempt at reconstruction and further development can be successful if it is not accompanied by attempts to establish a just and lasting peace, not only between Iran and Iraq, but also in the Persian Gulf as a whole.

Given the above, in the third part, we shall put foward certain recommendations which, if adopted, we would expect to provide the necessary conditions for long-term development and stability in the area.

Economic consequences of the war: a summary

As noted throughout this study, the economic consequences of the war on Iran and Iraq have been catastrophic, to say the least. However, although, as observed, Iran's infrastructure has suffered most, it should not be forgotten that, at the time of the invasion, Iran, as a result of the revolution, had already been subjected to chaos and economic disorder, while Iraq was at its 'apex of development' with a promising future ahead of it. Thus, when the impact of the war on Iraq is the subject of analysis, the above observation should not be underestimated.

To recall some of the more important points established in this study, it can be seen that, as far as Iran is concerned, the most damaging consequence of the war has been the failure of the Islamic Republic to reverse the Shah's policies and bring any tangible positive changes in the economic direction of the country.

As noted, the revolution had promised to reduce Iran's dependency on oil revenues, diversify the economy, increase non-oil exports, reduce Iran's dependency on trade with the West, make agriculture the 'axis of development', increase food/agricultural production, reduce consumer-goods imports and finally put an end to the rural–urban migration.

Throughout this study these issues were addressed, discussed and analysed. The changes since the revolution/war were noted. It was established that, in all cases, the situation has become much more problematic and intensified. We noted that, as the revolution was a popular mass movement, then the chances were that, if not all the objectives of the revolution, at least some of them could have been achieved by now.

To reduce Iran's military expenditure (Milex), as noted, was another major promise by the revolutionary leaders. Indeed it was observed that in the first two years before the Iraqi invasion, the new government in Tehran, adhering to their promise, rapidly and significantly reduced Iran's Milex and arms imports.

However, since the invasion, both Milex and arms imports as well as the corresponding defence and arms-import burdens have all increased rapidly and significantly.

In all, it can be said that the failure to realize any of the economic and defence expenditure objectives of the revolution and to part with the past policies can be identified as one of the most serious consequences of the war.

The war correspondingly has had a devastating impact on Iraq. It was noted that there has been a very serious deterioration in all aspects of the economy, with oil production/exports and revenues suffering most. We also established that, since the war, there has been a massive increase in Iraq's import dependency, as well as a major deterioration of the agricultural sector, leading to a great reduction in food production and consequently causing a major rise in agricultural import-dependency.

As for Iraq's Milex since the war, it was shown that, although there has been a major decline in Iraq's GDP since the invasion, none the less there has been a rapid increase in military expenditure, resulting in an unparalleled rise in the country's defence burden.

We also noted that, since the war, there has been a huge increase in the number of people under arms in Iraq. In fact, it can be argued that Iraq has been turned into a military machine, as the percentage share of the total population involved with the armed forces has increased from 1.7 per cent in 1979 to 17 per cent in 1987.

In this book we also attempted to demonstrate the world's hypocrisy and double standards in so far as the sales of arms to areas of conflict, i.e. the Iran–Iraq war, are concerned.

We noted that there has been hardly a country in East or West, South or North, where the rules of the game have not been allowed to be broken, so that weapons could be exported or re-exported to one or both countries.

It was established that, during the first part of the war (i.e. 1980–3), there were 26 countries supplying all kinds of weapons to Iran and Iraq. This figure had, however, increased to 41 by the end of the second period (i.e. 1983–6).

We also observed that the Gulf War has led to the rise of a few prominent Third World arms exporters, in particular China and Brazil, who have developed a thriving arms-export business because of the war. It was argued that, as long as the war continues, there exists an easy and ready market for outside penetration. However, this might not necessarily be the case whenever the war ends and should Iran and Iraq return to their more traditional arms suppliers, to purchase the best weapons and not the second-best ones. The consequences of such an action on Brazil and China could be profound, to say the least.

Furthermore, as was noted, Turkey has also become a major trading partner of both Iran and Iraq since the war began, exporting civilian goods and services and importing vast quantities of oil in exchange.

We argued that, while Turkey has been receiving oil from Iran and Iraq, she has been selling to them goods and services which might not have been sold elsewhere, i.e. in the West, with such ease.

Moreover, it was contended that trade of this kind must have been highly advantageous to Turkey, leading to a great improvement in her foreign-exchange earnings and economic well-being.

However, when the war ends, it was argued, should Iran and Iraq decide to curtail their trade with Turkey and spend their moneys on importing sophisticated technology and higher-quality goods and services from the West instead, then the result could be a serious blow to Turkey's economy, with some major consequences.

In all, it was argued that, if the above scenarios should happen, peace might bring economic hardship or even instability to those countries that have greatly benefited from the war and have become dependent on trade with the warring nations in the Gulf. Peace might bring many changes in war-time trading and friendship.

In this book we also attempted to demonstrate the impact of the revolution in Iran, the consequent rise of Shi'ite fundamentalism in largely Sunni-dominated countries in the Gulf, and the war on the pattern of military expenditure and arms imports in Saudi Arabia and Kuwait.

It was noted that, since the early 1980s, there has been a significant rise in Milex, both in absolute and relative terms in these countries. It was established that a major share of such increases in Milex has been on imports of major sophisticated weapon systems, mainly from the USA, France and the UK.

It was also established that, since the war began, the figure for military manpower in Saudi Arabia and Kuwait has significantly increased. In fact, the figures in both countries have increased by 5 per cent on average each year during the 1979–85 period, as opposed to 2 per cent during the pre-war period of 1973–8.

Therefore it can be argued that another major consequence of the war has been the further escalation of the militarization of neighbouring countries in terms of increases in their Milex, arms imports and the number of military personnel.

We also argued that, if Iran, Iraq, Saudi Arabia and Kuwait had agreed to limit their military expenditure to a level representing a 4.5 per cent defence burden each year since the first oil-price increase of 1973/4, then, by 1986, they could have accumulated a combined sum of $436.3 billion in their foreign-exchange reserves.

It was then suggested that the above sum could have been turned into capital for the creation of the potential Gulf World Development Bank to foster, promote and finance development projects in the Third World.

Finally, in this book, we attempted to bring together the various component parts of the economic cost of the war to Iran and Iraq.

We estimated that the total economic cost of the war to Iran, from 1980 to August 1988 (in current prices) was $644.3 billion and to Iraq $452.6 billion. These were the purely monetary costs of the war to both countries and did not include losses through inflation, the deaths of hundreds of thousands of the working population, the depletion of natural resources, the halt to crucial development, the interruption training and education and welfare payments to the hundreds of thousands injured in the war who can no longer contribute fully to the national economy.

We also noted that, although the economic costs of the war to Iran and Iraq's economies are very close, none the less a major difference exists in that, in the case of Iran, the total cost includes more actual costs, while in the case of Iraq, its total includes more opportunity costs. This was because, in the case of Iran, a much higher rate of actual damage to the infrastructure was assumed.

Finally, it was noted that the grand total economic cost of the war to both countries is the sum of $1,097 billion. In order to put this figure into better perspective, we noted that it exceeds by $678.5 billion the entire oil revenue received by both countries, ever since they started to sell their oil on the world market.

Destruction and reconstruction

From the analysis presented in the previous section, it becomes clear that Iran and Iraq face a gigantic task of reconstruction of their war-damaged economies and regions.

Reconstruction must start soon after the cessation of hostilities in order to allow the homeless and displaced population to return to their places of origin, to raise the hopes and faith of the affected masses, to prevent problems from building up and multiplying and, finally, to move towards a more normal life.

The scale of destruction has presented the planners and policy-makers with an unparalleled opportunity to change or formulate new policies and introduce strategies to bring about changes in the physical and socio-economic structure of the countries concerned that would not have been possible otherwise.

However, the need for immediate action should not justify and legitimize unplanned and unco-ordinated policies or projects. Lack of planning would undoubtedly lead to the risk of chaos, waste, duplication and socio-political instability (note the outcome of unplanned and unorganized policies in Iran after the 1973–4 oil-price increases).

Immediately after a disaster public officials almost always speak of making things better than ever before and of rebuilding the city better than it ever was. But, if this is to happen, how should these and other promises be delivered?

It is striking to note that, given the frequent occurrence of disasters, man-made or natural, and the ensuing destruction, there are very few comparative studies in reconstruction.[1] However, the existing literature indicates that reconstruction after a disaster is an orderly and predictable process (Hass *et al.* 1977: xxvi). For example, towns and cities are rebuilt on the same sites, while the pre-disaster trends, i.e. population and rural/urban growth, continue during the reconstruction period, and dominant economic sectors or social groups continue to be dominant (Amirahmadi 1987: 141).

Trends tend to continue and are reinforced by two powerful factors: uncertainties about the future for those who live and work in the city, and the bias of the existing institutions in restoring the pre-disaster, i.e. pre-war, order (Hass *et al.* 1977: xxvi).

In all, the central issues and decisions are value choices that give varying emphasis to an early return to normality, the reduction of future vulnerability, opportunities for improved efficiency, equality and amenities.

The post-disaster/war reconstruction process/recovery can be divided into four different but somewhat overlapping periods/stages. They are: emergency, restoration, replacement and developmental reconstruction (Hass *et al.* 1977). The rate of recovery during each stage is varied and depends on the extent of the actual damage, the availability of resources, the conditions during the pre-disaster period, the degree of planning comprehensiveness, and such qualities as leadership, management and bureaucratic efficiency (Hass *et al.* 1977: xxviii and 142).

The emergency stage is the immediate period after the occurrence of a disaster, e.g. bombardment or a missile attack. Depending on its severity, the disaster leaves behind problems caused by destruction and a large number of dead, injured, homeless and missing people.

At this stage normal social and economic activities are disrupted. Given the community's ability to recover, this period may last only days or a few weeks. The cessation of search and rescue and a massive reduction in emergency feeding/housing marks the end of the emergency period.

The restoration period begins during the final part of the emergency operations. It is marked by the patching-up of public utilities, housing, industrial and commercial structures which can be restored and the return to more normal social and economic activities.

The end of this period is marked by the return of major urban services, transport and utilities, the return of those evacuees wanting to return and substantial rubble removal. The completion period of this stage is generally 20 to 30 times longer than that of the emergency period.

The replacement/reconstruction period aims to restore the city's destroyed capital stock of various types (including buildings, bridges, roads and highways) to a pre-disaster level. At this stage, reconstruction, rather than patching up or coping as far as one is able, is emphasized. However, it should be noted that, during this period, activities are limited to restoring what has been destroyed, rather than to the creation of anything new.

During this period, regular planning, as opposed to the emergency programmes of the previous two stages, becomes essential. The replacement period is 100 to 150 times longer than the emergency period, and five to eight times longer than the restoration period. While self-help activities and motivations are fundamental to a speedy recovery and the successful completion of the first two periods, the replacement stage requires increased government assistance and intervention.

The final stage, namely developmental reconstruction, is primarily concerned with the improvement of existing (or pre-disaster) activities, organization and structure, and also with the creation of new ones, leading to further growth and development.

Large-scale projects should be carefully planned and evaluated to reflect people's needs and available or easily obtainable resources. Such projects, by their nature, are government financed. Self-help activities lose their importance in such projects, although they remain in supporting small-scale projects in and out of the city.

Activities during this final period should be directed to furthering material goods and objectives and should adhere to the sectoral mix and regional balance of reconstruction strategies. Development reconstruction is generally two or three times longer than the replacement reconstruction period.[2]

Reconstruction activities in Iran and Iraq have so far been largely limited to the first two periods and early parts of the third stage. Therefore the main and the most important task of rebuilding the war-damaged areas remains to be started and completed in future years.

The actions taken in these areas are directly affected by nationwide decisions, and thus they will undoubtedly influence the outcomes of national policies. This is to say that the objectives of post-war reconstruction and national goals must be compatible and reinforce each other.

The following goals of national policy, amongst others, which have been identified by both countries in the past, are particularly sensitive to the type and strategy of reconstruction, and the quality of its outcome:

1 Export diversification and less dependency on oil revenues.
2 Reduction of reliance on foreign technology.
3 Increase in agricultural productivity and reduction of reliance on food imports, with the ultimum goal of self-sufficiency in future.
4 Provision of the basic needs for all, in the areas of education, health care, housing, food and clothing.
5 The efficient use of scarce resources.
6 Creation of an integrated national settlement system.
7 Elimination of unemployment.

These material goals and objectives will, one way or another, direct the style, and therefore most profoundly influence the realization of post-war policies. The achievement of these goals will be enhanced by policy and the strategy of industrialization and modernization in the post-war era.

Given the outcome of unsuitable policies in the past and present we recommend an immediate change in industrialization policy and the adoption of a new and more suitable strategy.

We recommend that planners and policy makers in Iran and Iraq should adopt an appropriate technology policy of industrialization, not only in the war-damaged areas, but also in the rest of their countries as a whole.

The adoption of such a strategy which relies on indigenous techniques, using local resources, will lead to the realization of many national/post-war reconstruction goals, such as the reduction in dependency on oil revenues, reduced reliance on foreign technology, the efficient use of scarce resources, increased employment and reduction in rural–urban migration.

We should, at this point, emphasize that we are not arguing that countries like Iran and Iraq should eliminate the use of modern, externally produced technology. What we are suggesting is the adoption of a balanced mix of technologies, leading to a two-tier technology policy: the use of advanced techniques in heavy and large-scale industries, and the use of intermediate and traditional technology in light industries and small-scale production.

The many advantages of adopting such a policy have been discussed at some length by the present author elsewhere, and, therefore, we do not attempt to elaborate on them any further here (Mofid 1987: chapter 9, 267–75).

In all, it must be said that, given the hardship endured by the people of both countries, the principles of social justice and economic development should guide the respective governments in their policies of post-war reconstruction. They should also devise measures for redistribution of income and wealth amongst the population. The main concern, in the short run at least, should be the provision of basic needs for all.

An important question at this point should be, how is the reconstruction going to be financed? Financial resources for post-war reconstruction may be mobilized in various ways. The most important source, given that Iran and Iraq are major oil-exporting countries, seems to be their oil revenues.

However, the crash in oil prices, accompanied by a huge surplus in oil supplies, has meant that Iran and Iraq, for many more years to come, cannot expect an oil revenue higher than $7 billion to $9 billion each year (if we assume no further drastic fall in oil prices occurs).

Such a low level of expected future income is hardly enough to finance imports of food and other essential commodities, let alone to enable Iran and Iraq to start the huge task of reconstruction. If the shortage of money is going to be a major obstacle to reconstruction, what are the possibilities for other resources to be mobilized? The following recommendations are expected to go a long way towards removing the financial constraints on post-war reconstruction.

1 Self-help: the sale of 'reconstruction loan drive' bonds by the two governments to their respective nationals.
2 Regional help: the setting up of a 'regional grant reconstruction drive'. Grants to be given to Iran and Iraq by the countries in the region, especially by Saudi Arabia and Kuwait. As noted in chapter ten, these two countries have financed Iraq's 'engine of war' with $0.5 billion per month during the 1980–6 period. Why should they not be expected to finance the post-war reconstruction of Iran and Iraq by the same amount each month? This is only logical, if they want peace and stability in the region.
3 International help. The setting up of an 'international low interest, long-term loan reconstruction drive'. As noted in this study, the major arms suppliers have been directly or indirectly the main beneficiaries of the war, fuelling the engine of destruction in Iran and Iraq. Now is the time to expect them to finance the engine of reconstruction in these countries.
4 Japan and South Korea will be among those benefiting most from post-war reconstruction. They should also join the proposed international reconstruction drive, by providing financial assistance to Iran and Iraq.

All in all, nothing short of a Marshall-type plan of reconstruction is needed for Iran and Iraq to enable them to start the task of rebuilding.

Measures to enhance peace and stability in the region

As noted before, no attempt at reconstruction and furthering development can be successful if it is not accompanied by attempts to establish a just and lasting peace, not only between Iran and Iraq, but also in the region as a whole. Indeed, given the present power of destruction that comes with today's war technology, lasting reconstruction and redevelopment are possible only under the condition of a lasting peace.

As a first step towards the establishment of conditions necessary to bring about stability and peace in the region, we suggest an immediate action to reduce the burden of high military expenditure in the Gulf countries. This recommendation adheres to the understanding that the high levels of Milex and arms imports by the developing countries of the Third World has decreased rather than increased the sense of security and stability in these countries.[3]

Furthermore, given the rapid decline in oil prices in the last few years and with no forecast of any significant price rises in the near future, now, more than ever before, there exists a serious opportunity cost, even in major oil-exporting countries of maintaining a high rate of defence burden. Indeed today the 'haves' as well as the 'have nots' are facing the 'guns vs. butter' dilemma.

However, in order to reduce the level of Milex and to stop the arms race in the region, with a view to demilitarizing the Gulf, as a minimum the following conditions must first be met.

1 The acceptance by the countries in the region of 'Principles to guide mutual relations' among the countries concerned.
2 Recognition of the invisibility of frontiers. This implies a definitive recognition of the state frontiers and renunciation of all territorial claims.
3 Respect for the sovereign equality of the participating states.
4 Prohibition of the use or threat of force against the territorial integrity of states.
5 Non-intervention in the internal or external affairs of other states.
6 Non-assistance to terrorist or other subversive activities directed against the regime of another state (on these issues see Goldblat 1987: 3).

In order to increase the credibility and legitimacy of these principles, they *must* be enshrined in a declaration signed at the highest political level and have a comparable force to that of an international treaty.

In order to further the conditions of peace and stability,

these principles must then be underlined with a certain series of confidence-building measures. These measures should include:

1 Withdrawal of troops from border zones, leaving police forces only.
2 Establishment of 'hot-line' communication systems to reduce the likelihood of an outbreak of hostilities in the region by accident or misunderstanding.
3 Notification of any significant changes introduced or planned in the military sector (Goldblat 1987: 3).

The above measures must then be accompanied by other confidence-building actions in other areas. For example, there should be:

1 A serious attempt to increase trade and business between the states concerned. An economic interdependency is one of the most effective measures for reducing the possibility of war. Note, for example, what has happened since World War II in and between the European Economic Community, the USA and Japan.
    Therefore we recommend the establishment of the Gulf Heads of States Yearly Economic Summit to discuss their bilateral trade and to further the possibility of an eventual economic integration.
2 Introduction of cultural exchanges and measures to increase interstate travel by the nationals of the states concerned.
3 Provision of measures to promote most seriously the learning of Farsi in the Arab countries of the Gulf and Arabic in Iran.

If there is unreserved acceptance of these principles and confidence-building measures by the states concerned, the next logical step for their successful implementation is to give them an international stamp of approval.

Furthermore, as noted clearly in this book, the main arms suppliers are the ones who have benefited most from the militarization of the Gulf. Without their agreement and co-operation in reducing the flow of arms to the area, we can expect no mitigation of crisis and no serious chance of a successful 'get together' by the Gulf countries themselves.

Given the seriousness of the problems, we recommend the establishment of an international conference to limit the transfer of conventional arms to the Persian Gulf. The conference, which should include the USA, Soviet Union, UK, France and China, as well as the Gulf countries themselves, should make policies and recommendations on how to reduce the value and volume of arms exports to the region.

The above suggestions and recommendations on the style and strategy of reconstruction, as well as the provision of measures and policies to bring about peace and security in the region, constitute the groundwork necessary for the reconstruction of Iran and Iraq.

Their adoption does not promise the attainment of impossible goals but will enhance the establishment of a just and lasting peace in the region, without which any reconstruction and development will, sooner or later, be again a journey into destruction.

Appendix

Abbreviations used in tables listing weapons, weapon systems and other military equipment

AA	Anti-aircraft
AAG	Anti-aircraft gun
AALC	Amphibious assault landing craft
AAM	Air-to-air missile
AAV	Anti-aircraft vehicle
AC	Armoured car
Acc to	According to
ADV	Air defence version
Adv	Advanced
AEV	Armoured engineering vehicle
AEW	Airborne early-warning system
AF	Air Force
ALCM	Air-launched cruise missile
Amph	Amphibious vehicle/amphibian aircraft
APC	Armoured personnel carrier
ARM	Anti-radar missile
ARV	Armoured recovery vehicle
AShM	Air-to-ship missile
ASM	Air-to-surface missile
ASSV	Assault vehicle
ASuM	Air-to-submarine missile
ASW	Anti-submarine warfare
ATM	Anti-tank missile
ATW	Anti-tank weapon
AV	Armoured vehicle
BL	Bridge-layer
Bty	Battery

COIN	Counter-insurgency
CPC	Command post carrier
ECM	Electronic countermeasures
EW	Electronic warfare
FAC	Fast attack craft (missile/torpedo-armed)
FSCV	Fire support combat vehicle
Hel	Helicopter
ICV	Infantry combat vehicle
IDS	Interdictor/strike version
Incl	Including/includes
Landmob	Land-mobile (missile)
LAV	Light armoured vehicle
LSH	Heavy-lift ship
LST	Tank landing ship
LT	Light tank
Mar patrol	Maritime patrol aircraft
MBT	Main battle tank
MG	Machine-gun
MICV	Mechanized infantry combat vehicle
Mk	Mark
MoU	Memorandum of understanding
MPWS	Mobile protected weapon system
MRCA	Multi-role combat aircraft
MSC	Minesweeper, coastal
MSO	Minesweeper, ocean
MT	Medium tank
PC	Patrol craft (gun-armed/unarmed)
Port	Portable
Recce	Reconnaissance (aircraft/vehicle)
Repl	Replenishment
RL	Rocket launcher
SAM	Surface-to-air missile
SAR	Search and rescue
SC	Scout car
ShAM	Ship-to-air missile

ShShM	Ship-to-ship missile
ShSuM	Ship-to-submarine missile
SLBM	Submarine-launched ballistic missile
SPG	Self-propelled gun
SPH	Self-propelled howitzer
SSBN	Nuclear-powered, ballistic missile-equipped submarine
SShM	Surface-to-ship missile
SSM	Surface-to-surface missile
SuAM	Submarine-to-air missile
Sub	Submarine
SuShM	Submarine-to-ship missile
TD	Tank destroyer
TG	Towed gun
TH	Towed howitzer

Notes

Chapter one

1 The literature on historical, military and religious/cultural aspects of the conflict is indeed voluminous. The following provide a sample of such coverage: J. M. Abdulghani 1984; R. C. Johansen and M. G. Renner 1985; P. Marr 1985; S. Tahir-Kheli and S. Ayubi 1983; W. O. Staudenmaier 1983; C. Wright 1985; MERIP 1984; E. Karsh 1987, 1988; A. Cordesman 1984; R. King 1987; S. Chubin 1986; G. Nonneman 1986; Foreign Policy Association (1985a); W. Goldstein 1984; J. A. Bill 1984; D. Ross 1984.

2 In contrast to the socio-political, historical and military analysis of the Gulf War which, as note 1 describes, has received voluminous coverage, the economic consequences of the conflict, on the other hand, have received scanty coverage. For example, the only study known to the present author which has attempted to estimate the economic cost of the Gulf War is by Abbas Alnasrawi (1986). Other studies that have somehow dealt with some aspects of the economic impact of the war include J. Townsend 1984; Keith McLachlan and George Joffè 1984, 1987; T. Stauffer 1985; and also short articles by different reporters in publications such as the *Financial Times*, *Wall Street Journal*, *Middle East Economic Digest* (MEED) and *Middle East Economic Survey* (MEES). It should also be noted that the two publications by McLachlan and Joffè, although detailed and credit-worthy, were written by non-economists. It seems that, once again, the economists have, by and large, virtually ignored the study of wars. Rosen (1968 in G. Harris 1986) regards this as 'the most important abdication of any' by economists. For evidence on this statement see G. Harris 1986. However, at least not all the economists, it seems, have ignored this topic. E. Kanovsky (1970) and R. W. Stevens (1976) are the most noted ones.

3 For evidence on the figures quoted, see M. Yamaoka 1987.

4 For an excellent reading on this statement see John G. Stoessinger 1987.

5 For the English text of the agreement see the *New York Times*, 8 March 1975.

6 The 1937 Agreement contained two major provisions: first, in designating the low-water mark on the eastern bank of the Shatt al-Arab as the frontier, it conferred control over the waterway on Iraq with the exception of the area adjacent to the Iranian ports of Abadan, Khoramshar and Khosrowabad where it was fixed at the *thalweg* (the deep-water line); and second, as a result of that demarcation, it provided that vessels in the Shatt should employ Iraqi pilots and fly the Iraqi flag (again with the exception of these three areas in which the boundary was determined by the *thalweg*). For further reading on these issues see Karsh 1987.

7 On these issues see further Stephen D. Goose 1987: chapter 8.

8 For an excellent account of the purges of the Iranian armed forces see W. F. Hickman 1982.

Chapter three

1 By the end of 1985 only 24 per cent of the economically active population was engaged in agriculture as opposed to 30 per cent in 1980. For evidence see FAOa 1985.

Chapter four

1 Militarization as used here refers to a process in which increasing state resources are allocated to the armed forces and/or military-related activities. Militarism, according to A. Vagtas (1957) refers to a preference or bias favouring military force, institutions, symbols and rituals which may be manifested by civilians as well as military men. Similarly anything beyond the scientific application of necessary resources for external defence is defined as militaristic. For further reading see Wolpin 1983: 129–55.

2 The exchange rates were as follows: $1 = rials 68.9 (1973), 67.6 (1974), 67.6 (1975), 70.2 (1976), 70.6 (1977) and 70.5 (1978).

Chapter five

1 For evidence on the formation and development of the Revolutionary Guard Corps see IISS 1987/8.

Chapter six

1 The exchange rates during the period under study were as follows: $1 = 0.30 dinars (1973) and 0.29 (1974–8).

Chapter eight

1 The interested reader in following this topic could consult the following works amongst others: COPAT 1978; *Links* 1983; IDS 1985; Eccles 1983; N. Harris 1983; Jolly 1979; Kaldor and Eide 1980; McMahan 1984; United Nations Department for Disarmament Affairs 1982a.

Chapter nine

1 For an excellent study of opportunity costs of military expenditure see David Dabelko and James M. McCormick 1977: 145–54.
2 For an excellent reading on 'action/reaction' model see L. F. Richardson 1960.

Chapter ten

1 See chapter 1, notes 1 and 2.
2 The actual rate of interest used in our calculations is the US certificate-of-deposit rate which was 13.97 per cent in 1980, 15.91 per cent (1981), 12.35 per cent (1982), 9.09 per cent (1983), 10.37 (1984), 8.05 (1985) and 6.8 (1986).
3 For an excellent reading on Kuwait's overseas portfolio, see 'Kuwait comes out buying', *Business Week*, 7 March 1988.
4 It is important to note that the most frequently used Defense Department estimates of the budgetary cost of the Vietnam War are all in current prices covering a span of years in which average prices paid by the federal government rose some 65 per cent. See further Stevens 1976: 178–9.

Chapter eleven

1 The following list of references demonstrates this very clearly: Jack Hirschleifer 1963; Bates *et al.* 1963; Ciborowski 1969; Dacy and Kunreuther 1969; Douty 1969; Kates *et al.* 1973: 981–90; Cochrane 1974; Rosental 1974; Hass *et al.* 1977; Amirahmadi 1987: 134–47.
2 For further reading on different stages of reconstruction see Hass *et al.* 1977: xxv–xxxv and 141–2.
3 For further reading on these and other related issues see Goldblat 1987: 1–4; Ball 1983: 507–27; Faini, Annez and Taylor 1984: 487–98; Thorsson 1983: 113–17; Aben 1986; Arlinghaus 1984; Bisinas and Ram 1986; COPAT 1978; IDS 1985; *Links* 1983; N. Harris 1983; Mofid 1987.

Bibliography

Abdulghani, J. M. (1984) *Iraq and Iran: The Years of Crisis*, London: Croom Helm.

Aben, J. (1986) 'The French Socialists confronted with the problem of arms exports', *Defence Analysis*, 2, 4.

Algermissen, S. T. *et al.* (1972) *A Study of Earthquake Losses in the San Francisco Bay Area: Data and Analysis*, Report prepared for Office of Emergency Preparedness, National Oceanic and Atmospheric Administration, Washington, DC: US Department of Commerce.

Ali, S. R. (1984) 'Holier than thou: the Iran–Iraq war', *Middle East Review*, 17, 1.

Alnasrawi, A. (1986) 'Economic consequences of the Iraq–Iran war', *Third World Quarterly*, 8, 3, July.

Amirahmadi, H. (1987) 'Destruction and reconstruction: a strategy for the man-damaged areas of Iran', *Disasters*, 11, 2.

Arlinghaus, B. (1984) *Military Development in Africa: The Political and Economic Risks of Arms Transfers*, Boulder, CO: Westview Press.

Arms Control and Disarmament Agency (annually) *World Military Expenditures and Arms Transfers*, Washington, DC: Arms Control and Disarmament Agency.

Axelgard, F. W. (1988) *A New Iraq: The Gulf War and the Implications for US Policy*, London: Greenwood.

Ball, N. (1983) 'Defence and development: a critique of the Benoit Study', *Economic Development and Cultural Change*, 31, 3, April.

Bani-Sadr, A. B. (1978) 'Instead of the Shah, an Islamic Republic', *New York Times*, 11 December.

Bates, F. L. *et al.* (1963) *The Social and Psychological Consequences of a Natural Disaster: A Longitudinal Study of Hurricane Audrey*, Disaster Study No. 18, Washington: National Academy of Sciences Printing Office.

BBC (1982) 'Iranian oil supply and future oil export policy', *Summary of World Broadcasts (SWB)*, London: British Broadcasting Corporation, 16 November.

Behdad, S. (1988) 'Foreign exchange gap, structural constraints and the political economy of exchange rate determinations in Iran', *International Journal of Middle East Studies*, 20, 1.

Bibliography

Bill, J. A. (1984) 'Resurgent Islam in the Iraq–Iran war', *Foreign Affairs*, 63, 1.

Bisinas, B. and Ram, R. (1986) 'Military expenditures and economic growth in less developed countries: an augmented model and further evidence', *Economic Development and Cultural Change*, January.

BP (annually) *Statistical Review of World Energy*, London: British Petroleum.

Brown, J. and Snyder, W. P. (eds) (1985) *The Regionalization of Conflict*, New Brunswick, NJ: Translation Books.

Brzoska, M. (1987) 'Profiteering on the Iran–Iraq war', *Bulletin of Atomic Scientists*, June.

Brzoska, M. and Ohlson, T. (1986) *Arms Production in the Third World*, London: Oxford University Press.

Business Week (1986) 'Who keeps the Gulf War going?', 29 December.

Cannizo, D. (1980) *The Gun Merchants: Politics and Policies of the Major Army Suppliers*, New York: Pergamon.

Central Bank of Iran (annual) *Annual Report and Balance Sheet*, Tehran: Central Bank of Iran.

Chubin, S. (1986) 'Reflections on the Gulf War', *Survival*, July–August.

Chubin, S. and Tripp, C. (1988) *Iran and Iraq at War*, London: I. B. Tauris.

Ciborowski, A. (1969) *Warsaw, a City Destroyed and Rebuilt*, Warsaw: Interpress.

Cochrane, H. C. (1974) 'Predicting the economic impact of earthquakes' in Cochrane, H. C. *et al.* (1974) *Social Science Perspectives on the Coming San Francisco Earthquake: Economic Impact, Prediction and Reconstruction*, Natural Hazards Research Working Paper No. 25, Boulder, CO: University of Colorado.

COPAT (1978) *Bombs for Breakfast*, London: Committee on Poverty and the Arms Trade.

Cordesman, A. (1984) *The Gulf and the Search for Strategic Stability*, Boulder, CO: Westview Press.

Cordesman, A. (1987a) 'Arms to Iran: the impact of US and other arms sales on the Iran–Iraq war', *American Arab Affairs*, 20.

Cordesman, A. (1987b) 'The realities and unrealities of the Middle Eastern arms market', *RUSI [Royal United Services Institute] Journal*, 132, 1.

Dabelko, D. and McCormick, J. M. (1977) 'Opportunity costs of defence: some cross-national evidence', *Journal of Peace Research*, 14, 2.

Dacy, D. C. and Kunreuther, H. (1969) *The Economics of Natural Disasters: Implications for Federal Policy*, New York: Free Press.

De Bock, W. and Deniau, J.–C. (1988) *Des Armes pour l'Iran*, Paris: Gallimard.

Development and Peace (quarterly), various issues.

Disarmament, various issues.

Douty, C. M. (1969) 'The economics of localized disasters: an empirical analysis of the 1906 earthquake and fire in San Francisco', unpublished PhD dissertation, Stanford University, Department of Economics.

Dussauge, P. (1985) *L'Industrie Francaise de l'Armament*, Paris: Economica.

Eccles, P. (1983) *Disarmament and Development: The Vital Links*, Dublin: Irish Commission for Justice and Peace.

The Economist (weekly), various issues.

EIU (Economist Intelligence Unit) (1984) 'Iran', *Quarterly Economic Review*, 2.

El Azhary, M. S. (ed.) (1984) *The Iran–Iraq War: An Historical, Economic and Political Analysis*, London: Croom Helm.

Etelaat (daily, in Farsi), various issues.

Faini, R., Annez, P. and Taylor, L. (1984) 'Defence spending, economic structure and growth: evidence among countries and over time', *Economic Development and Cultural Change*, 32, 3.

FAOa (annually) *FAO Production Yearbook*, various issues, Rome: Food and Agricultural Organization.

FAOb (annually) *FAO Trade Yearbook*, various issues, Rome: Food and Agricultural Organization.

Financial Times (daily), various issues.

Foreign Policy Association (1985a) 'The Iran–Iraq war: the war as others see it' *Great Decision '85*, New York: Foreign Policy Association.

Foreign Policy Association (1985b) 'The Gulf, the war and the US policy', *Great Decision '85*, New York: Foreign Policy Association.

Goldblat, J. (1987) 'Demilitarization in the developing world', *Journal of Peace Research*, 24, 1.

Goldstein, W. (1984) 'The war between Iran and Iraq: a war that can't be won or ended', *Middle East Review*, 17, 1.

Goose, S. D. (1987) 'Armed conflicts in 1986 and the Iran–Iraq war' in SIPRI (1987) *Yearbook on Armament and Disarmament*, Stockholm: Stockholm International Peace Research Institute.

Grummon, S. R. (1982) *The Iran–Iraq War: Islam Embattled*, CSIS Washington Paper No. 92, New York: Praeger.

Guardian (daily), various issues.

Guardian, Washington Post, Le Monde (weekly), various issues.

Harris, G. (1986) 'The determinants of defence expenditure in the ASEAN countries', *Journal of Peace Research*, 23, 1.

Harris, N. (1983) *Of Bread and Guns: The World Economy in Crisis*, Harmondsworth: Penguin.

Hass, J. E., Kates, R. W., and Bowden, M. J. (eds.) (1977) *Reconstruction Following Disaster*, Cambridge, MA: MIT Press.

Helms, C. M. (1984) *Iraq: Eastern Flank of the Arab World*, Washington, DC: Brookings Institution.

Hickman, W. F. (1982) *Ravaged and Reborn: The Iranian Army*, Washington, DC: Brookings Institution.

Hiro, D. (1984) 'Chronicle of the Gulf War', *MERIP Reports*, July–September.

Hiro, D. (1989 forthcoming) *The Longest War: Armed Conflict between Iran and Iraq*, London: Grafton Books.

Hirschleifer, J. (1963) *Disaster and Recovery: A Historical Survey*,

Memorandum RM-3079-PR, prepared for the United States Air Force Project Rand, Santa Monica, CA: Rand Corporation.

Hoogland, E. (1984) 'The Gulf War and the Islamic Republic', *MERIP Reports*, 14, 6–7, July–September.

IDS (1985) 'Disarmament and world development: is there a way forward?', *IDS Bulletin*, 16, 4, University of Sussex, Institute of Development Studies.

IISS (annual) *The Military Balance*, London: International Institute for Strategic Studies.

IMFa (annual) *International Financial Statistics*, various issues, Washington, DC: International Monetary Fund.

IMFb (annual) *Direction of Trade Statistics Yearbook*, various issues, Washington, DC: International Monetary Fund.

International Herald Tribune (daily), various issues.

Jane's Defence Weekly (weekly), various issues.

Johansen, R. C. and Renner, M. G. (1985) 'Limiting conflict in the Gulf', *Third World Quarterly*, 7, 4.

Jolly, R. (ed.) (1979) *Disarmament and World Development*, Oxford: Pergamon.

Kaldor, M. and Eide, A. (eds) (1980) *World Military Order*, London: Macmillan.

Kanovsky, E. (1970) *The Economic Impact of the Six-Day War*, New York: Praeger.

Karsh, E. (1987) 'The Iran–Iraq war: a military analysis', *Adelphi Papers*, No. 220, spring.

Karsh, E. (1988) 'Military power and foreign policy goals: the Iran–Iraq war revisited', *International Affairs*.

Kates, R. W., Hass, J. E., Amaral, D. J., Olson, R. A., Ramos, R. and Olson, R. (1973) 'Human impact of the Managua earthquake disaster', *Science*, 182.

Kayhan (daily, in Farsi), various issues.

Kazerooni, M. R. (1985) *Negareshi no be Mohazerat Dar Iran* [A New Look at Internal Migration in Iran], Tehran: Centre for Rural Research and Agricultural Economy.

King, R. (1987) 'The Iran–Iraq War: The Political Implications', *Adelphi Papers*, No. 219.

Klare, M. T. (1980) 'Military madness', *The New Internationalist*, September.

Klare, M. T. (1986) 'The state of the trade', *Journal of International Affairs*, 40, 1.

Links (1983) 'Disarmament-development', No. 18, Oxford: Third World First.

Litwak, R. (1981) *Security in the Persian Gulf: Sources of Inter-state Conflict*, London: Gower.

McLachlan, K. and Joffè, G. (1984) *The Gulf War: A Survey of Political Issues and Economic Consequences*, London: Economist Intelligence Unit.

McLachlan, K. and Joffè, G. (1987) *Iran–Iraq: The Next Five Years*, London: Economist Intelligence Unit.

McMahan, J. (1984) *Reagan and the World: Imperial Policy in the New Cold War*, London: Pluto.

McNaugher, T. L. (1985) *Arms and Oil: US Military Strategy and the Persian Gulf*, Washington, DC: Brookings Institution.

Marr, P. (1985) *The Modern History of Iraq*, Boulder, CA: Westview Press.

MEED (weekly) *Middle East Economic Digest*, various issues.

MEES (weekly) *Middle East Economic Survey*.

MERIP (1983) 'The arms race in the Middle East', *Middle East Reports*, No. 112.

MERIP (1984) 'The strange war in the Gulf', *Middle East Reports*, Nos. 125/126.

MERIP (1987) 'Re-flagging the Gulf', *Middle East Reports*, No. 148.

Mofid, K. (1987) *Development Planning in Iran: From Monarchy to Islamic Republic*, Wisbech, Cambs.: MENAS Press.

New York Times (daily), various issues.

Nonneman, G. (1986) *Iraq, the Gulf States and the War*, London: Ithaca Press.

The Observer (weekly), various issues.

OECD (quarterly) *Oil and Gas Statistics*, Paris: Organization for Economic Co-operation and Development, various issues.

Ohlson, T. and Skons, E. (1987) 'The trade in major conventional weapons', *Yearbook on Armament and Disarmament*, Stockholm: Stockholm Peace Research Institute.

OPEC (annually) *OPEC Annual Statistical Bulletin*, Vienna: Orangization of the Petroleum Exporting Countries.

Palme, O. *et al.* (1982) 'Military spending: the economic and social consequences', *Challenge*, September–October.

Perkins, K. (1980) 'The death of an army: a short analysis of the Imperial Iranian Armed Forces', *RUSI [Royal United Services Institute] Journal*, 125, 2, June.

Petroleum Economist (monthly), various issues.

Pierre, A. J. (1981–2) 'Arms sales: the new diplomacy', *Foreign Affairs*, 60, 2 (winter): 226–86.

Pierre, A. J. (1982) *The Global Politics of Arms Sales*, New York: Council Foreign Relations.

Plan and Budget Organization (1982) *First Five-Year Economic, Social and Cultural Development Plan, 1983/1984–1987/88*, Tehran: Islamic Republic of Iran.

Republic of Iraq (1983) *Annual Abstract of Statistics*, Baghdad: Ministry of Planning, Central Statistical Organization.

Richardson, L. F. (1960) *Arms and Insecurity*, Chicago, Ill.: Boxwood Press.

Rosen, R. (1968) in Harris, G. (1986) 'The determinants of defence expenditure in the ASEAN countries', *Journal of Peace Research*, 23, 1.

Rosental, J. C. (1974) 'Redevelopment after a natural disaster: a planning strategy for recovery', unpublished BA thesis, University of Cincinnati.

Ross, D. (1984) 'Soviet views towards the Gulf War', *Orbis*, 28, 3.

Sanger, C. (1985) *Safe and Sound: Disarmament and Development in the 1980s*, London: Zed Press.

Simpson, J. (1988) 'Along the streets of Tehran: life under Khomeini', *Harper's Magazine*, January.

SIPRI (Stockholm International Peace Research Institute) (annual) *Yearbook on Armament and Disarmament*, London: Taylor & Francis.

Sivard, R. (annual) *World Military and Social Expenditures*, World Priorities.

Statistical Centre of Iran (1983) *Iran Reflected in Statistics*, Tehran: Statistical Centre of Iran.

Statistical Centre of Iran (1985) *Large Manufacturing Establishments' Statistics: Results of the 1984 Survey*, Tehran: Statistical Centre of Iran.

Statistical Centre of Iran (1986, 1987) *A Statistical Reflection of Islamic Republic of Iran*, Tehran: Statistical Centre of Iran (March 1986 and July 1987).

Statistiques (annual) *Statistiques de l'Industrie Petrolière (Pétrole)*, Paris, various issues.

Staudenmaier, W. O. (1983) 'A strategic analysis' in Tahir-Kheli, S. and Ayubi, S. (eds) (1983) *The Iran–Iraq War*, New York: Praeger.

Stauffer, T. (1985) 'Economic warfare in the Gulf', *American-Arab Affairs*, 14.

Stevens, R. S. (1976) *Vain Hopes, Grim Realities: The Economic Consequences of the Vietnam War*, New York: New Viewpoints.

Stoessinger, J. G. (1987) *Why Nations Go to War?*, 4th edn, London: Macmillan.

Stork, J. (1981) 'The war in the Gulf', *MERIP Reports*, 11, 5, June.

Tahir-Kheli, S. and Ayubi, S. (eds) (1983) *The Iran–Iraq War*, New York: Praeger.

Thorsson, I. (1983) 'Guns and butter: can the world have both?', *International Labour Review*, 122, 4, July–August.

Tower Commission Report: The Full Text of the President's Special Review Board, New York: Bantam Books.

Townsend, J. (1984) 'The war: the economic consequences for the participants' in El Azhary M. S. (1984) *The Iran–Iraq War: An Historical, Economic and Political Analysis*, London: Croom Helm.

Turkuje Sinai Kalkinma Barkasi (1983) *Agricultural Machinery: Country Report: Iraq*, Istanbul: A. S. Export Promotion Programme.

United Nations (1982) *The Relationship between Disarmament and Development*, Report to the Secretary-General, New York: United Nations.

United Nations (1983) *Economic and Social Consequences of the Arms Race and of Military Expenditure*, New York: United Nations.

United Nations (1985) *Making the Connection: Disarmament, Development and Economic Conversion*, New York: United Nations.

United Nations (1986) *Statistical Abstract of the Region of the Economic Commission for Western Asia*, 9th issue, Baghdad: United Nations.

United Nations (annual) *Economic and Social Survey of Asia and the Pacific*, various issues.

United Nations (annual) *Statistical Yearbook for Asia and the Pacific*, various issues.

United Nations (annual) *Yearbook of National Accounts Statistics*, various issues.

United Nations Committee for Trade and Development (annual) *Handbook of International Trade and Development Statistics*, various issues.

United Nations Department for Disaramament Affairs (1982a) 'The relationship between disarmament and development', *Disarmament Study Series*, 5, New York: United Nations.

United Nations Department for Disarmament Affairs (1982b) *Repertory of Disarmament Research*, Geneva: United Nations.

United Nations Department of International Economic and Social Affairs (annual) *Yearbook of Industrial Statistics*, various issues.

United Nations Department of International Economic and Social Affairs (annual) *Yearbook of International Trade Statistics*, various issues.

United Nations Department of International Economic and Social Affairs (annual) *Yearbook of World Energy Statistics*, various issues.

United Nations Economic and Social Commission for Western Asia (1986a) *National Account Studies*, Bulletin No. 8, October, Baghdad.

United Nations Economic and Social Commission for Western Asia (1986b) *Statistical Abstract of the Region of the Economic Commission for Western Asia*, 9th issue, Baghdad.

USACDA (annual) *World Military Expenditures and Arms Transfers*, Washington, DC: United States Arms Control and Disarmament Agency.

Vagtas, A. (1957) *A History of Militarism*, New York: Free Press.

Washington Post (daily), various issues.

Wolpin, D. (1983) 'Comparative perspective on militarization, repression and social welfare', *Journal of Peace Research*, 20, 2.

Wright, C. (1980–1) 'Implications of the Iraq–Iran War', *Foreign Affairs*, 59, 2, winter.

Wright, C. (1985) 'Religion and strategy in the Iraq–Iran war', *Third World Quarterly*, 7, 4.

Yamaoka, M. (1987) 'Continuing fall of US crude oil production and growing dependence on imports', *JIME Review*, 10.

Index